LIVERPOOL BLITZED

SEVENTY YEARS ON

NEIL HOLMES

HALSGROVE

Dedication

This book is dedicated to my parents, who gave me a love of history from an early age, and Julia Hoffman as without her ongoing support, advice and encouragement this book would never have been published.

First published in Great Britain in 2011

British Library Cataloguing-in-Publication Data
A CIP record for this title is available from the British Library

ISBN 978 0 85704 079 4

Halsgrove
Halsgrove House,
Ryelands Business Park,
Bagley Road, Wellington, Somerset TA21 9PZ
Tel: 01823 653777   Fax: 01823 216796
email: sales@halsgrove.com

Part of the Halsgrove group of companies
Information on all Halsgrove titles is available at: www.halsgrove.com

Printed and bound in the U.K. by the MPG Books Group

Foreword

THE BOOK you are holding gives a fascinating and unique local insight into a period when Britain faced the greatest danger in its entire history – the Second World War. Several architectural gems and familiar civic landmarks were seriously damaged or completely destroyed by enemy action, and today there is a stark but poignant reminder of the Liverpool Blitz in the form of St Luke's church, which was purposely left by the post-war authorities to stand as a hollow shell after its interior was destroyed and gutted by a German incendiary bomb that fell upon it on the night of 5 May 1941. What else in Liverpool remains as a reminder of those far-off days when the Luftwaffe wreaked Blitzkrieg havoc on Liverpool and the realistic threat of German invasion hung over the nation? Not much. We have the Cenotaph on Lime Street, which commemorates the dead of both wars, the odd plaque or memorial (such as the one in Blackstock Street) to those who perished in the raids, and, for those who know where to look, we may see the pitted traceries of bomb-shrapnel scars on the sandstone walls of the Anglican Cathedral. But the Phoenix that is Liverpool has long arisen, reborn from the infernos of that apocalyptic period, which started with the German invasion of Poland and ended with the atomic annihilation of two Japanese cities.

Liverpool has grown, and expanded since World War Two, and with the passing of each generation, the personal recollections of those who remember the Liverpool Blitz will soon pass away into the relative obscurity of the dusty history book. Already, the conspiracy theorists are questioning whether NASA put twelve astronauts on the Moon. I personally saw the history-making broadcasts from the lunar surface live on television, but those who were not alive in the era of the Apollo Programme may find it easy to disbelieve that a dozen men have walked on the face of the Moon, just as some equally self-deluding 'revisionists' have even denied that the Holocaust took place. Perhaps the historians and the educationalists need to bring the past into present somehow, so that the people of today can get a perspective on what might otherwise seem a distant and dreary history lesson.

I believe books such as this one - *Liverpool Blitzed-70 Years On* – are the way to go. This one will certainly bring the reality of the Liverpool Blitz alive to modern eyes in a way that has rarely been seen before. The author Neil Homes takes the reader on a tour of blitzed Liverpool by comparing his excellent modern photographs of our 21st century city with archival monochrome images showing the stark aftermath from those hell-fire nights when Germany's Air Force attempted to destroy the morale of the Liverpool people along with their homes, places of work and entertainment, as well as sites of strategic importance. When I was a child my mother would often tell me about the night a factory in Edge Hill suffered a direct hit during the infamous May Blitz, and how she, as a child, watched the flaming margarine running like lava down the gutters of Angela Street. Only now, since reading Neil Holmes's book, have I taken the trouble to visit the street where this incident occurred.

I also looked at the corner on nearby Melville Place to see the tell-tale cemented cracks in the Minster Court apartment building, where a German bomb killed an entire family when it struck several corner flats in what was then the Myrtle Gardens tenements. Weeks before the tragedy, my grandmother had been given the very council flat the bomb had destroyed, but couldn't enter it because a recalcitrant lock prevented her entry.

Being a superstitious woman, she interpreted the faulty lock as an omen and decided to seek alternative accommodation, thus unknowingly saving the lives of herself and her family. On this same corner, on the borders of Toxteth and Edge Hill, my father emerged from an air-raid shelter in 1941 and for the first time in his life he saw two dead men, slumped over the controls of an anti-aircraft gun. Besides them, hanging over railings was the corpse of a stray dog with no insides. It had been killed by the same bomb that had killed the ant-aircraft gunners. The scene gave my father nightmares for weeks. I had heard these stories and many others as a boy, but after reading this book, the reality of the Liverpool Blitz finally 'came home' to me, and instead of merely reading about it, I truly understood the scale of devastation and appreciated the bravery of men and women of seventy years ago who died and suffered so I could live in a free country.

Tom Slemen

Acknowledgements

UNLESS OTHERWISE mentioned below the historical images are the copyright of the Liverpool City Record Office who kindly gave permission for their use in this book. I must also thank the staff at the Liverpool Record Office for their advice and help in locating information and press cuttings on Liverpool's wartime experiences. Without their expertise this book would have been impossible. Finally I wish to thank the author Tom Slemen for his support, advice and foreword.

The images on pages 37, 66 and both images on page 104 are reproduced with the permission of Scouse Press. The image on page 118 on the lower right of the page is reproduced by permission of Liverpool Anglican Cathedral. The image on page 99 is part of the E. Chambre Hardman Collection and is reproduced with the permission of the National Trust.

I have attempted to locate the copyright owner for the historical images on the following pages without success, but would be pleased to hear from them so that proper acknowledgement can be made: 17, 18, 19, 31, 42, 46 (right), 44, 57, 60, 73, 76, 77, 80, 82, 97 (top right) 101, 103, 124, 130, 131, 133 (both), 134 and 152.

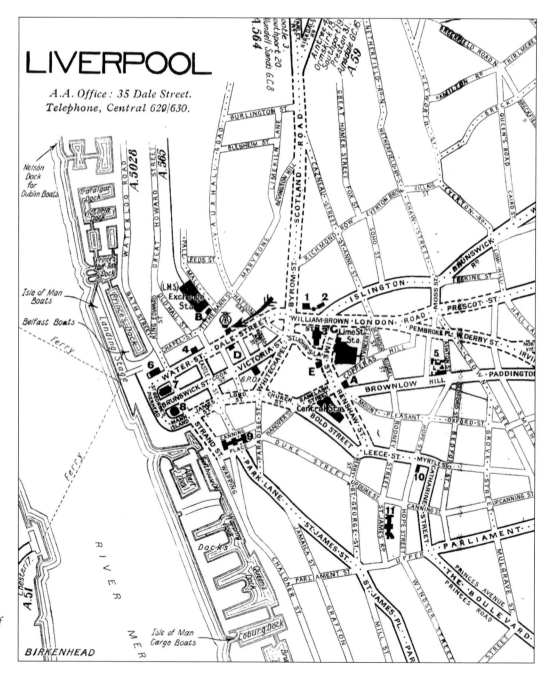

A detailed map showing s most of the major roads in the city centre.

Introduction

MANY BOOKS have been written about the experience of Liverpool during the Second World War. But as each passing year brings regeneration and development the visible scars of the war heal over. For most of us it is becoming all but impossible to relate to pictures of the damage caused by the Luftwaffe, since these pictures frequently show buildings long since demolished, or docks that no longer see ships.

This book is an attempt to rectify this by comparing photographs taken during the war with a modern photograph showing as similar a viewpoint as possible. By studying the images in this book people can get a feel for how the attacks changed the city forever. We must also not forget however that each image will tell a personal story.

Liverpool is sometimes said to have been the hardest hit city outside of London yet the port remained open providing a vital link in the Allied supply chain and playing a crucial role in the Battle of the Atlantic. In the Merseyside region it is thought that around 4,000 people died, 10,000 houses were destroyed and 184,000 damaged. In Liverpool alone 2,596 people were seriously injured and 1,600 lightly injured. For this reason I wished to show not just the city centre but images from the suburbs, to show how individuals and families could be torn apart overnight.

It is my sincere hope that this book will help people appreciate what the population went through and realise how grateful we should be to them.

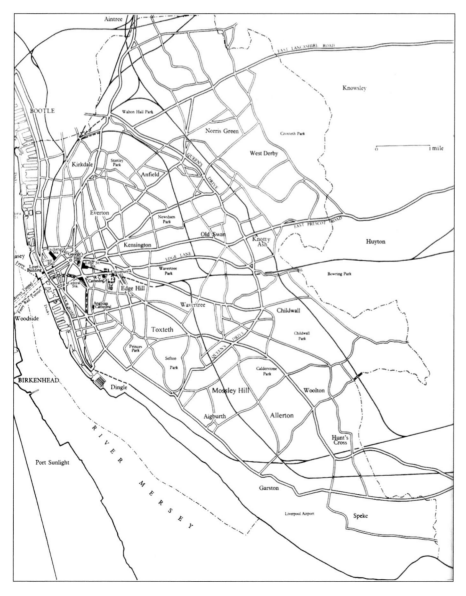

Liverpool and the surrounding area

Why Liverpool?

THE LIVERPOOL of 2011 would make an unusual target for an enemy attack. But the Liverpool at the outbreak of war in 1939 was a very different place. Liverpool was often referred to as the Empire's second city and had over 7 miles of quays and some 130 individual docks. Its extensive dock system also had over 100 miles of railway owned by the Mersey Docks and Harbour Board. Despite unemployment and economic difficulties in the 1930s the city still had a crucial role to play in the coming conflict. Britain was reliant on imported food and material required to conduct the war. Later the city was a transport hub for around 4.7 million Allied soldiers.

Some 55 million tons of imports passed through Liverpool's docks and warehouses during the war. The Germans' main aim was to hinder these imports and it was hoped that this, combined with the Battle of the Atlantic and attacks on other ports like Belfast and Glasgow would starve Britain into submission. By damaging the warehouses they could not only destroy recently arrived goods, but also hinder a dock's ability to store goods that were often perishable. By hitting the Overhead Railway they could undermine the speed at which personnel could move along the docks. By damaging rail communications they could inflict delays on goods coming off the convoys being delivered to the rest of the country.

Sadly for Liverpool and all the other cities which suffered air attack during the Second World War bombing methods in 1939 were hardly precise in daylight and wildly inaccurate at night. Due to the high casualties inflicted by the RAF during daylight operations almost all of the Luftwaffe's efforts against the city came at night. Liverpool also had large housing areas near the docks and close to the city centre which meant that even near misses could destroy a shop, church or group of homes. The British press at the time called some attacks "terrorism" raids and spoke of bombs which fell on civilian targets as if the Luftwaffe was doing so on purpose. In reality there was never any such intention, Liverpool was a victim of its own success and suffered for being a crucial cog in the machine that produced the Allied victory.

How it all Began

AROUND 11am on the 3rd September 1939, the Prime Minister, Neville Chamberlain broadcast to the nation that Britain was declaring war on Germany in response to the latter's invasion of Poland two days earlier. The British and French governments, concerned at the aggression of Adolf Hitler's Nazi regime had undertaken to defend Poland in the event of invasion. But their promise to Poland was ignored by Hitler, who felt that the previous appeasement policies made by the two countries would continue. Hitler's fatal gamble would lead to tens of millions of people losing their lives in a conflict that would engulf the world for the nearly six years.

Suddenly air raid sirens sounded over Liverpool. Like other British cities most of the children had been evacuated a few days earlier in the run up to war being declared but the city still contained hundreds of thousands of people. Fortunately the sirens were just a false alarm - it would be some time yet before the German Air Force (Luftwaffe) would appear over the city. After Poland was defeated the war settled into a phase known as the "phoney war" with neither side launching any major operations until April 1940.

For Liverpool things were not quite as simple. The city had fallen on hard times during the depression years of the 1930s. The war however was to change this overnight as the city with its enormous dock system became of vital importance to the war effort. The city became a destination for large convoys and a base for the Royal Navy ships that would protect them. Knowing this the Germans would naturally have considered the docks and city to be a fairly high priority target.

In June 1940 the war took on an entirely new aspect with the German invasion of France and the Low Countries. With the surrender of France and evacuation of Dunkirk the Germans soon controlled air bases in Northern France and were able to raid deeply into Britain, especially at night when they were harder to detect. Shortly afterwards the raids on Merseyside began, with the first fatality occurring on the night of the 9th August 1940 in Prenton (an area of Birkenhead), as a bomb fell through the roof of a house killing a maid. Few could guess that within less than two years the city and region would be transformed, with much of the city centre reduced to rubble and thousands made homeless. For Liverpool, the war had begun.

Timeline

Where two dates are given this represents a raid which started in the evening and went on through the night.

1939

3rd September	Britain declares war on Germany, Merseyside has its first air raid warning – a false alarm.

1940

27th June	The first bombs fall on Merseyside in a field.
July	Throughout the month sporadic raids continue but little damage is caused.
8th/9th August	A stick of high explosive bombs falls on Birkenhead. One lands on a house in Prenton killing a maid sleeping there.
17th/18th August	High explosive bombs are dropped on the southern docks area.
19th/20th August	Incendiary bombs land on the West Derby area of the city.
27th August	Two raiders appear over the city but little damage is done.
28th August	A heavy raid which mostly damaged residential property outside the city centre, the church of St Mathew and St James, Mossley Hill is badly damaged.
30th/31st August	A mixture of high explosive and incendiary bombs rain down on the Everton area, Mill Road Hospital is particularly badly hit.
31st/1st September	A night of three raids on the city. The Custom House is hit for the first time, Cleveland Square shelter is hit and over 100 small fires are reported.

Two examples showing damage to Mill Road Hospital after the later raid on the 3rd May 1941.

3rd/4th September	Incendiary bombs shower the Kensington, Ullet Road, Lark Lane and Aigburth Vale areas.
4th/5th September	The Edge Hill and Lister Drive districts are hit hard in a medium sized enemy raid.
5th/6th September	The first appearance of oil bombs causes major damage to houses in the Walton and St James Road areas. Everton FC's ground, and the Anglican Cathedral are damaged.
10th/11th September	High explosive bombs fall in the West Derby and Woolton areas, houses in Speke are also badly damaged.
11th/12th September	The Gatecre area is hit by incendiary and high explosive bombs.
12th/13th September	Langton Dock and Wellington Road, Wavertree are hit in a two hour raid.
14th September	A single raider causes slight damage to Gladstone and Alexandra Docks.
15th/16th September	The Anfield, Fairfield, Walton and Norris Green areas are attacked, later Great Homer street is attacked.
17th September	In an evening raid Garston and Speke is hit by raiders.
18th/19th September	Walton Prison is hit on a night when over 1000 high explosive and 500 incendiaries are dropped.
21st/22nd September	TJ Hughes Department store, Central Station and Alexandra Dock are hit.
23rd/24th September	Walton is particularly badly hit in a heavy raid.
24th/25th September	A night of two raids during which the Stanley Dock Warehouse is hit.
26th/27th September	Most of the southern docks are badly damaged along with the Cunard Buildings and Mersey Docks and Harbour Board Buildings.
27th/28th September	A night of three attacks during which Garston and Great Homer Street areas are hit.
29th/30th September	Dingle, Aigburth and Everton areas are badly hit.

A badly damaged secondary school pictured in September 1940.

1st October	Two enemy aircraft bomb East Toxteth Dock causing minor damage.
2nd October	A minor raid hits the Kensington area.
7th/8th October	The first raid for three nights hits the Wavertree, Great Mersey Street and Stanley Road areas. A large number of incendiaries fall in Sefton Park to little effect.
9th October	A Junkers 88 bomber is brought down near Bromborough Dock.
10th October	Much of the suburbs are hit by raiders dropping incendiary and high explosive bombs.
11th October	The area around South John, Paradise, Red Cross, James and Hanover Streets are badly hit.
13th/14th October	More than 40 bombers attack the city in a raid lasting 4 hours, damaging docks and houses.
16th October	Five planes cause damage to the Everton area.
17th October	Extensive damage is caused to houses and a hospital in the West Derby area.
18th October	Norris Green area is badly hit.
19th October	The Dingle area is badly damaged in a raid.
21st October	Incendiary bombs cause heavy damage across the city.
22nd October	A single raider drops bombs that kill 4 children buying tickets outside a cinema.
23rd October	A ten hour raid which marked Liverpool's 200th alert but thankfully caused relatively minor damage.
25th October	Houses and a school are damaged in the Richmond Park area.
26th/27th October	Netherfield Road area is badly hit.

Two examples of damage done during October 1940, below to a Church School, right to a block of flats.

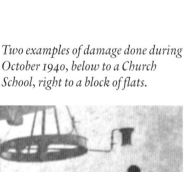

29th October	Queen's Dock is badly hit.
29th/30th October	Warehouses in the Thomas Street and South Castle Street areas are hit along with the telephone exchange on South John Street. Bryant and May's match factory in Garston is set on fire.
1st November	County Road, Great Howard Street and East Lancashire Road area is hit.
4th/5th November	Townsend Avenue and Wavertree playground are hit.
8th/9th November	Incendiaries fall in the Childwall Valley Road area.
10th/11th November	22 aircraft attack the city causing minor damage.
12th November	Edge Hill goods station is hit along with a post office in Wavertree Road.
18th November	Sefton and Guest Streets are hit.
19th November	Aigburth is badly hit along with three houses in Anfield.
23rd November	A lone raider drops bombs on Great George Street.
29th November	Liverpool's first major attack and the first time the enemy used parachute mines against the city. A gas holder in Garston is hit by a bomb and only heroic efforts save the area. A basement shelter in Durning Road collapses killing 166 people. Extensive damage is done throughout the city.
30th November	A lone raider drops bombs in the Rathbone Road area.

Houses in Circular Road, Norris Green narrowly missed by a bomb.

Police search through damaged buildings for some of their comrades

20th December	After three weeks of light raids with no damage the Luftwaffe returned with a vengeance. Fifty raiders attack the city over nearly 10 hours. Damaged buildings include the Town Hall, Municipal Buildings, Cunard Building and Exchange Station.
21st/22nd December	150 bombers arrive over the city badly damaging the northern docks, Hanover Street, Hatton Garden, the Royal Infirmary and St George's Hall. The Leeds-Liverpool Canal is also breached in a raid that made extensive use of parachute mines.
23rd December	A light attack damaged Huskisson, Langton and Alexandra Docks.
24th December	Raids continue this night but most bombs fell in the river.

Conference near damaged houses in the Edge Lane area during the January raids.

A street shelter demolished during the December raids.

1941

1st January	The New Year is seen in with a small raid that caused minor damage.
8th January	After a lull in raids the city is attacked by 200 aircraft which drop bombs on the south docks, damaging houses and warehouses alike. Everton area is also hit.
15th February	A month of minor raids with this night being the worst with the north end of the city hit.
12th March	After some reconnaissance flights over the city earlier in the month this night saw the return of heavy raids. Some 126 fires were dealt with including one at the Head Post Office in Victoria Street. South John Street Telephone Exchange, the Cotton Exchange and Municipal Annexe on Dale Street are also hit.
13th March	Alexandra Dock sheds are badly damaged in a light raid.

One of the more prominent victims of the May Blitz, Lewis's Department Store.

14th March	Speke is hit along with Kirkby railway station.
15th March	The Mammoth floating crane is sunk in Birkenhead Docks
7th April	75 raiders attack the city damaging the Beaconfield Road area. Lister Drive power station is hit again.
15th April	A light raid with little damage.
26th April	A high explosive bomb damages a babies' home.
1st May	Start of the "May Blitz", Liverpool's darkest time but a relatively light raid. Lime Street station is temporarily closed by damage.
2nd/3rd May	SS *Malakand* is set on fire in Huskisson Dock during a raid that sees heavy damage across the city.
3rd/4th May	Liverpool's worst night. The SS *Malakand* explodes in Huskission Dock showering debris over an area of up to a mile. Damaged buildings include the museum and public libraries on William Brown Street, the Rotunda Theatre, Lewis's and Blackler's stores, the Bluecoat Chambers, Anglican Cathedral, St Luke's church on Leece Street and St Michael's church on Pitt Street. Hundreds of people were killed or injured in this raid alone.
5th and 6th May	Attacks relatively light but the city struggles to cope with the extensive damage and fires caused by the raid on the 4th.
7th May	Heavy raid which caused more serious fires to break out in the dock area.
8th May	Scattered raids shower the city with incendiaries but cause few casualties.
28th May	A light raid by three bombers which did little damage.
30th May	A small raid which badly damaged the Mersey Docks and Harbour Board Offices and the Corn Exchange on Fenwick Street. By the end of May 1,453 people had been killed and 1,065 seriously injured in Liverpool alone.

A U-Boat enters Gladstone Dock on 17th May 1945 as part of the German surrender terms.
On board was a German crew, Royal Navy escort and a Mersey River pilot.

June	Minor raids towards the end of the month with little loss of life or damage caused.
July	Another quiet month punctuated by raids on the 6th and 24th when surface shelters were damaged.
August and September	Two more quiet months with raiders being seen but only scattered bombs dropped.
October	There were raids on the 12th, 20th, 22nd and 26th but very little damage or loss of life.
2nd November	A light raid causes some losses.

1942

10th January	The final raid on the city demolishes houses in Upper Stanhope Street. Ironically one of them (102) was once the home of Adolf Hitler's half brother Alois.

1945

30th April	Adolf Hitler commits suicide in a bunker in Berlin as the Allied armies encircle the city. His Third Reich outlives him by barely a week bringing an end to the war in Europe.
15th August	After the dropping of atomic bombs on Hiroshima and Nagasaki Japan surrenders ending the war in the Pacific. Liverpool's war is finally over.

A street party to celebrate the end of the war. Sadly for those present rationing would remain for many years yet!

Around the Pierhead

WHETHER IT be the River Mersey or the seas and oceans beyond, Liverpool is forever linked to water and there are few places where this is clearer than around the Pierhead. You only have to look at the splendour of the Liver Buildings, the Cunard Building or the Port of Liverpool Building in the photograph above to appreciate what wealth and confidence that link could produce. Together they still form an unforgettable view and a major part of why the city was awarded the status of a World Heritage Site in 2004.

No city can be a time capsule though, and the area has seen extensive change since the war, making some of the views that follow initially difficult to relate to. Perhaps the greatest loss was the Overhead Railway which closed in 1956 but other casualties include the Custom House, Corn Exchange and the Goree Piazzas. Given how heavily the city was bombed however we are fortunate that most of the major buildings in this area survived without extensive damage.

This recent photograph shows the Pierhead as it appears today, with the famous Three Graces in the background. In the foreground is the recently opened canal section which links the Albert Dock to the Leeds-Liverpool Canal.

The Pierhead is also home to a number of memorials relating to the sacrifices and contributions made by sailors from Britain, the Commonwealth and Europe to winning the Second World War.

On a wall close to the Liver Buildings is this plaque erected in 1944 as a record to the unity of the US and

UK authorities in moving goods through the port during the Second World War. There is also a statue to Captain Frederick "Johnny Walker", a famous U-Boat hunting ace. He spent a great deal of the war based out of Gladstone Dock but sadly died at the age of 48 in 1944 when he suffered a blood clot, probably due to overwork and exhaustion. This statue is seen below in front of the Museum of Liverpool Life on the left and the memorial to the 1,390 Merchant Navy men who lost their lives whilst serving with the Royal Navy on the right.

Another memorial is shown above and is dedicated to those members of the Merchant Navy killed in both world wars. In the background is the Port of Liverpool building. In front of this is a line of maple trees which were planted in memory of Canada's contribution to the Battle of the Atlantic.

This photograph shows the Three Graces in the background on the right and in the foreground a part of the Overhead Railway that has been demolished by a high explosive bomb. This was the world's first electric elevated railway and ran along the length of most of the city's dock system. Opened in 1893 it provided a speedy method of transport for dock workers who nicknamed it the "Dockers' umbrella". On the right can just be seen the corner of one of the Goree Piazzas. The presence of so many bystanders and the fact that such an important road has not yet been cleared of debris suggests that this photograph was taken only shortly after the raid that caused this damage.

The modern view shows a sign of the times, with the railway being replaced by a widened dock road (known in this area as the Strand). In the background the Pierhead buildings provide a good reference point for the comparison. The taller building on the far right is the iconic Liver Buildings. Next to this is the shorter Cunard Building, once the home of the shipping line with the same name. The next building to the left is a ventilation tower for the Mersey Tunnel. Just above the modern temporary office building is the dome of the Port of Liverpool Building. The city is fortunate that these buildings survived the war intact given the damage to the nearby Overhead Railway and other buildings. The Port of Liverpool Building was hit but was repaired without any noticeable external difference.

Pictured here in front of the Liver Buildings is a Republic P-47 Republican Thunderbolt. Although an American plane it was also used by the RAF amongst others. In the background can also be seen Tower Building and just behind it India Buildings. Legend says that if the Liver Birds ever flew away the city of Liverpool would cease to exist. It was perhaps a daily comfort for locals to look up and see them sitting safe throughout the air raids.

Despite frequent modern alterations to this part of the Pierhead the main buildings still remain largely unchanged.

This photograph was taken in the part of Brunswick Street which runs between the Cunard Building (left) and Port of Liverpool Building (out of shot to the right). The former was built as the headquarters of the Cunard Steamship Company in 1916, with work going on even in the midst of World War One. One of the company's famous liners, RMS *Lusitania* was torpedoed and sunk off the coast of Ireland shortly after construction of the building began. Near the top of the building can also be seen the coats of arms of the United Kingdom's World War One allies. In 1919 the company's express liners had moved to Southampton but the headquarters remained here. By 1934 the company merged with the White Star Line whose headquarters were badly damaged during the war (see page 23). Although the bomb damage here was an inconvenience we are fortunate that it fell between the buildings rather than on one of them! During the war the lower basement of the building was used as an air raid shelter for those who worked in the nearby offices. It also provided the central Air Raid Precaution headquarters for the city.

Damage like this was usually repaired fairly quickly to avoid any prolonged transport problems. Today the Cunard Building is occupied by a number of public and private sector organisations. The Cunard shipping company followed the liners in the 1960s, ending more than 120 years of association with the port.

The Port of Liverpool Building was completed in 1907 and was the home of the Mersey Docks and Harbour Board. As can be seen here the eastern side of the building was badly damaged on the night of 2nd/3rd May 1941. Despite the extensive damage and fire the building's sound design allowed it to be repaired swiftly.

The Mersey Docks and Harbour Company moved out of the building in the 1970s. The building is now occupied by businesses.

from where the famous Mersey Ferries sailed. During the war two ferries, the *Oxton* and *Bebington* were fitted with cranes and used to offload planes mid river and deliver them to the Pierhead. A third ferry, *Upton* was taken over by the Army and used as a supply vessel for the anti-aircraft forts in Liverpool Bay.

Since the war the area between the Three Graces and the river has changed frequently. The Pierhead remained a terminus for public transport long after trams vanished but today mostly only sightseeing buses such as the one shown here visit. In the foreground can be seen a line of maple trees. These comprise a living memorial to the Canadian forces that fought and died in the Battle of the Atlantic. There are plans to add 18 apartments to the top floor of the Port of Liverpool Building, yet another example of how an old building is being converted to a use its wartime occupiers could never have conceived. A modern ferry terminal and landing stage have recently re-opened here bringing tourists back to a crossing with origins going back centuries.

Although taken long after the raids ended this photograph shows some of the air raid shelters constructed at the Pierhead to complement the large basement shelter contained beneath the Cunard Building. In the foreground can be seen tram lines, for the Pierhead was the terminus of many of the tram routes. To the right of this scene was the terminal

This photo shows the Dock Road between James Street and Water Street. It is initially unfamiliar since most people today do not think of this stretch being this narrow. During the Second World War however a set of buildings known as the Goree Warehouses ran down the centre of the Strand and appear on the left of this photo. The tall building in the centre of the photo is the Wellington Building and just beyond it stands Tower Building. The properties on the right which stood between Brunswick Street and the White Star Building on the corner of James Street were all demolished by enemy action.

After suffering considerable damage the Goree Warehouses were eventually demolished in the late 1940s and early '50s. They were initially replaced by a car park before eventually the area became a central reservation. New property has been built on the right hand side of the road but both the Wellington Building and Tower Building have survived.

This photo shows a similar section of the Dock Road to the previous page, but this time from near the Wellington Building looking towards James Street. It is quite likely to have been taken on the same day as the previous one as the same piece of metal/wood can be seen leaning against the central building on the left. The Goree Warehouses appear again, this time on the right side of the photo. In the distance on the left can be seen the former White Star Building. It was badly damaged by incendiary bombs on the night of 2nd/3rd May 1941. The roof of the building was especially badly burnt as can be seen here.

In the modern photograph the White Star Building (now known as Albion House) can barely be seen behind the newer buildings. As has already been said the Goree Warehouses were demolished after the war leaving this central reservation. Their demolition allows us a view towards Canning Dock which lies

just beyond the temporary construction on the right behind the traffic lights. Once again the angle of this shot was changed in order to avoid the heavy traffic on the Strand.

Our Lady and St Nicholas' church stands just across the Dock Road from the famous Liver Buildings in an area heavily hit by the air raids. On 21st December 1940 the main body of the church was destroyed by fires started by incendiary bombs. Books published during the war tended to refer to incidents such as this in terms of vandalism or question whether the subject of the photo was a "Military Objective?" as if the German bomb aimers were hovering over their sights keeping a special lookout for church spires or towers! As has been mentioned the reality was that inaccurate bombing methods meant that this kind of damage was all too frequent but entirely incidental.

In 1943 a temporary chapel was erected in the church grounds to continue services. No doubt at least partly because it was (and still is) the parish church of Liverpool the church was completely rebuilt after the war. Today it is still often known as the Mariner's Church and contains a chapel dedicated as part of the 50th anniversary celebrations of the Battle of the Atlantic in 1993.

Shortly after the raid a cross was fashioned from the remains of timber salvaged from the burnt-out church. This still hangs in the church today in the Chapel of St Peter which is named after the church which once stood in Church Street.

This photo shows the view up Brunswick Street from its junction with Drury Lane. The premises on the right are all that remains of the Corn Exchange building which was hit by high explosive bombs on the night of the 2nd/3rd May 1941. To add to the chaos a fire broke out in the remains turning the area into a burning nightmare. Remarkably three people who had hidden beneath one of the building's stairways were rescued. Rescue workers rarely gave up even after it was clear no more survivors could be found. Some rescue operations were only closed twelve days after the last body was recovered. The building in the distance in the background is a branch of the Bank of England on Castle Street which suffered a near miss during the war as shown on page 46.

Given its prominent location it will come as no surprise to see that the Corn Exchange site was built on after the war and is now a large office building with the same name. Most of the remaining buildings are still standing which is fortunate as serious fires often spread to nearby premises, meaning an incendiary bomb could often inflict damage out of all proportion to its relatively small size and weight. Because of this the city used a system of firewatchers, a team of whom would spend the night on lookout for any incendiaries and take prompt action to put out the fires the bomb started. It was a highly dangerous task and many of them died in air raids whilst on duty. Their brave service was a vital part of the city's defences and saved many buildings from being gutted.

This image of James Street Station aptly demonstrates the damage this area suffered. All that remains above ground was the decorative tower of the station with its water tank for the hydraulic system that was used to power the lifts. On the left is the rear of the White Star Building and in the background on the right is the Liver Buildings.

The tower was pulled down during the war and later replaced with this modern building. James Street was later incorporated into the Loop Line system connecting it to the other city centre stations and retaining its connection to the Wirral Line. The station now uses electric lifts.

platform level. The exit to Water Street was also blocked off by fires and damaged buildings in that area. Fortunately the fires remained at ground level keeping the civilians safe until an exit route could be established. The tall building in the centre of the image is the National Bank, and next to this is the former North and South Wales Bank, which at the time of the war was used for various offices. Just beyond this on the corner of Castle Street was a branch of the Midland Bank. The building on the right would have been the Mersey Tunnel Vaults which once sported an anchor for a pub sign! This photograph was taken in September 1941 and demonstrates that the damage inflicted on even important buildings could often take months to completely remove once the site had been made safe.

This view up James Street from the strand again demonstrates the extensive damage inflicted on James Street Station during the raids. The station once stood in the gap in the buildings on the left, along with two hotels and a restaurant. James Street was an underground station even then and its platforms were used as makeshift shelters on many nights. On the night of 3rd/4th May 1941 however fires in nearby buildings spread to the booking hall and damaged the lift system which was stuck at the

The changes to James Street Station were discussed on the previous page. Both the National Bank and the branch of Midland Bank later became bars, the former retaining its name whilst the later became the Trials Hotel. The former North and South Wales Bank was later renamed Castle Moat House since it stands on the moat for the long demolished Liverpool Castle. The Mersey Tunnel Vaults was later replaced by the Mersey Mission to Seamen. This was later converted back into a hotel and then a pub before closing again.

Liverpool's fifth Custom House stood in Canning Street, was designed by John Foster and was completed in 1839 on the site of the city's first dock. The building was over 470 feet long and contained the offices of the Board of Trade and the Excise Office along with its own post and telegraph offices. The building was badly damaged on more than one occasion during the war. In August 1940 a high explosive bomb damaged the glass dome in the centre of the building and fires did some damage to the roof. It was then hit on three consecutive nights starting on the 3rd/4th May 1941 during which

the fires completely gutted the building and left the glass from the dome hanging down in bizarre patterns.

Although the building was still standing when the war ended it was sadly demolished in the early 1950s to "create employment". It is a shame that the authorities did not create employment renovating the building, although it is difficult to imagine what use it would have been put to today. In its place now stands the newly opened Paradise Street bus station.

The tall building on the right, is the Merseyside Police Headquarters. Not far from here in the Liverpool One shopping centre a circular glass viewing window in the ground allows people to view foundations of the first dock which date back to 1715. This was the world's first commercial wet dock but was closed in 1826 and filled in two years later to enable the construction of the Custom House. This comparison shot was taken from a slightly different angle to allow a better view of the current site.

The Defenders

THE ROLE of protecting Liverpool from the Luftwaffe raids fell to a large number of organisations. Some of these such as the Home Guard and Air Raid Wardens will be familiar from TV shows such as *Dad's Army*, but others less so. The military played their role, providing anti-aircraft batteries and barrage balloons. These were primarily used against relatively low flying enemy planes, their main effect being to force the enemy raiders to bomb from a height at which bombing accuracy was limited even further. The Royal Air Force also provided fighter cover from airbases in Speke, Wrexham and Anglesey.

One of these was 312 Squadron, formed with Czechoslovakian pilots and based at Speke. It was pilots from this squadron that brought down the

Junkers 88 over Bromborough Pool (see page 90). They flew Hawker Hurricane fighter planes, an example of which can be seen above. The squadron's badge can be seen below left. The Junkers was the squadron's first aerial victory, shared between Flight Lieutenant Gillam, Pilot Officer Vasatko and Sergeant Stehlik. Gillam later drove to the crash site and cut two swastikas from the plane to keep as souvenirs.

The Czechoslovakian pilots had fled their home country after the German occupation, flying for the French Air Force then later the RAF. Along with Polish and French pilots they proved invaluable during the Battle of Britain.

No amount of fighter cover and anti aircraft fire can ever completely prevent a target from being bombed so the authorities needed some way of dealing with this. The Air Raid Precautions (ARP) was an organisation that had been set up in 1924, dedicated to finding ways of protecting the civilian population. Before the war it tended towards exaggeration, sincerely believing that there would be 65,000 casualties a week, starting almost as soon as war was declared. It also believed that civilian morale would crack and people would have to be forced to return to work each day. In reality during the whole war around 60,000 civilians were killed and morale remained remarkably high.

During the war the ARP was responsible for the issuing of gas masks, upkeep of public shelters and the maintenance of the blackout. The city was split up into 7 different sectors based on the Police Divisional Areas. Some women were also used as ambulance drivers. Most members were trained in basic first aid and casualty recovery. With a total force of around 1.4 million members across the country they played a vital role in the nation's defences.

If the authorities had overestimated the Luftwaffe's potential to annihilate the civilian population it underestimated what damage it could do to the city's buildings. The danger of fires started primarily by incendiaries dropped by the enemy's planes proved greater than anyone locally or nationally had believed. There had been some preparations such as the setting up of the Auxiliary Fire Service (AFS) in 1938 but it lacked a central organisation and standardisation of equipment. In Liverpool there were nearly 5,000 members, most of whom were unpaid part-timers.

The government had provided an extra 445 pumps to supplement the Fire Brigade's existing equipment. Initially it had been planned to have each pump responsible for its own small section of the city but this was dropped and 47 sector stations such as the one in Durning Road were used instead. The AFS was later replaced by the National Fire Service (NFS) which amalgamated local brigades with the AFS under one central organisation. Some firefighters can be seen in action above in St George's Crescent.

Above, members of the AFS enjoy a well earned tea-break on the 5th May 1941, no doubt after long days and nights fighting the fires that were still raging through the city.

It is perhaps some indication of just how severe the May Blitz was that 558 pumps were brought into the city by the 10th of May. The authorities did their best but some problems were just not that easy to resolve. The fast expansion of the fire services had caused problems in training and a lack of experience. Fire fighting was a complicated task even in peacetime conditions.

With the switch to the NFS in 1941 some of the problems were alleviated as more pumps were acquired, equipment was updated and emergency water supplies such as the one in Cook Street (page 46) were built. The sad irony is that most of these improvements came just as the German raids were coming to a end, a case of closing the stable door after the horse had bolted.

A crucial part of the city's defences was the relaying of messages from wardens to the service chiefs so that the response could be co-ordinated. This was done through telephonists in exchanges and control centres who often worked throughout the raids, dealing with emergency calls whilst bombs fell on the buildings around them. They were expected to be able to keep a clear head throughout, especially as they may well be receiving a call about bombs falling on an area where they or their relatives lived.

The police also played their role in protecting the city, reporting incidents, helping people into shelters, fighting incendiary bombs and generally helping to co-ordinate the local efforts. This was all done in addition to their normal duties of maintaining public order, a task exacerbated by the chaos caused by the raids. In this though they were assisted by members of the Home Guard and military. Many members of the Police Force were recognised for gallantry during the war.

Heroes

DURING THE war the local press gladly reported the exploits of people from the region who had been awarded medals for gallantry, either through service at home or in the forces. These reports provided relatives and the region alike with a source of pride and raised morale to know that people's efforts were not going entirely unnoticed. Such reports often lack details such as the location or precise date for fear that such information would have been put to use by the enemy.

The awards given to people from Merseyside varied from civilians being made an Officer of the Order of the British Empire (OBE) or awarded the George Cross to military awards such as the Distinguished Flying Cross (DFC), Distinguished Service Cross (DSC) or even the Victoria Cross (VC), the highest award any member of the armed forces can receive. There was even a wartime medal for animals known as the Dickin Medal. One of these was awarded to a Liverpool rescue dog known as Jet who was involved in search and rescue work in blitzed buildings. He is buried in Calderstones Park where there is also a memorial to him.

The following pages give but a small sample of the brave efforts that people of this region made. Many more people went about their duties without such official recognition but these provide a sample of acts both at home and abroad.

Captain William Eyton-Jones (right) who lived in Brodie Avenue was rewarded for the way he managed to save the lives of over 50 men. His ship was torpedoed by a submarine and sank in less than 3 minutes, leaving just a single life boat. He managed to make his way to this boat and took charge of searching for survivors and stores.

In all he managed to gather 58 men but precious little food or water. Undaunted he set a sail for friendly territory and ensured that the food was fairly rationed for the long journey, even though this meant only one cup of water and 2 bis-

cuits a day. When the tiny boat was picked up by a hospital ship after 13 days all but 2 men had survived the ordeal. During that time the boat had managed to make a quite astonishing 500 miles. The 47 year old was awarded an OBE, the citation for which talked of how he "showed high qualities of leadership and his seamanship never faltered".

Captain Eyton-Jones was a local man whose exploits took place in the words of the newspaper article "in a tropical sea" but plenty of heroic acts took place closer to home. Richard Bywater (below) was a Factory Development Officer at the Royal Ordnance Factory in Kirby. Built in 1941 the factory cost

He volunteered with three others to go through the stock one fuse at a time, isolating each defective one as it was found and moving it carefully to a safe area.

This was especially hazardous work since the fuses could be set off by vibration and the task took three whole days. One was so bad that it could not be moved far so he dismissed his helpers and then placed the fuse in an iron safe surrounded with sandbags before setting it off. This was highly dangerous work and he won the George Cross for it.

At 4am on September 1944 the factory once again suffered an incident. By this time its main role was filling bombs for the RAF and on that night there was a shattering explosion in one of the filling sheds. This started a major blaze which endangered the remaining bombs. Eight people were killed outright and another later died of the wounds received in this explosion. Firemen were called to the scene but they had to contend with exploding bombs and a raging fire. They managed to get one of the fires under control but another larger blaze broke out and by around dawn was threatening the entire site.

This larger fire was eventually brought under control but the shed was in a terrible state with a collapsed roof and the site was still dangerous. Richard Bywater was part of the team that worked on clearing the building and making the factory safe once more. For his role during this incident he was awarded the George Medal, making him the only civilian to ever receive both decorations. Almost a year later he was amongst a group of people who received their ribbon in a special ceremony at the factory, and two months later he received the medal from the King at Buckingham Palace.

£8,000,000 and by 1944 employed around 10,000 people who turned out 150,000 anti-tank fuses a week.

In the early hours of the 22nd February that year one of these fuses exploded, killing two female workers and injuring a third. Bywater quickly realised this was a major problem since the building where the explosion took place contained another 12,000 fuses, any number of which could also have been defective.

As can be seen on the previous page bravery was not the preserve of the armed forces and many civilians stepped forward at the city's hour of need. Many women volunteered to be ambulance drivers and faced the nightly perils of delivering injured people in the midst of an ongoing raid. One of these was Miss Christine Heard who lived in the Lark Lane area. During one particularly heavy raid she arrived at a demolished building were people were trapped and managed to direct the rescue of one of them who she drove to a nearby hospital.

Returning to the scene she found that the nearby roads were now blocked with AFS vehicles, unable to negotiate the roads due to fallen rubble. Despite bombs falling around her she offered to use her local knowledge to lead the AFS crews on an alternative route to the site of the worst fires. This done she carried on with her duties before reporting back to base for further duty. For her work that night she was awarded the British Empire Medal (BEM).

Members of the AFS were often faced with seemingly impossible situations but responded with bravery and skill. Two men, Fireman Alexander Conway and Fireman Edward Heyes were awarded a BEM for their work. During a raid in December 1940 they came upon the scene of 2 houses that had been demolished by a high explosive bomb. Working together Heyes supported a collapsed floor with his back whilst Conway worked a way further into the wreckage. Crawling through into an opening he had made he managed to rescue 5 women and a small child.

One final woman was buried in debris in a sitting position on a chair. Conway managed to free her using a saw to cut away at the chair arms. Throughout the whole incident there were bombs falling in the area and the streets were being subjected to machine gun fire. Matters were not helped by the fact that gas was escaping into the area from a fractured main, and fires were spreading in other areas. Both men were invested with their medals at Buckingham Palace on the 28th October 1941. This is in marked contrast to the briefing given to firemen at the start of the war which instructed them to only fight fires and to leave the rescue work to those with training. In practice this was not always possible.

One role sometimes overlooked was that of messengers which the AFS and NFS used extensively. Mostly teenage boys, they would carry messages throughout the city, usually using bicycles which were able to keep going through rubble strewn streets when a car or truck would be unable to get through. One messenger, Leo Broadbridge spent 12 hours on duty carrying messages between a crew and its station, for which he received the King's Commendation for Brave Conduct.

Home Guard

ON THE 14th May 1940 the Secretary of State for War, Anthony Eden made an announcement on the radio calling for the formation of Local Defence Volunteers from men aged 17-65 who were not already in military service.

Within a week police stations were inundated with a quarter of a million men. The formation that would become the Home Guard was born.

Our view of this organisation is clouded by sitcoms such as *Dad's Army* and in many respects comedy is only mirroring real life. In the early days the volunteers lacked uniforms, weapons and organisation beyond their locality. Fortunately many members had military experience from World War One and were able to add a backbone of knowledge and skills that would stand them in good stead in the weeks to come.

With the fall of France and the Dunkirk evacuations the threat of invasion increased the importance of the force. The British people responded with increased devotion and 1.5 million had volunteered by July. The name of the force was also changed to the more inspiring Home Guard. As the months passed the government were gradually able to provide equipment and uniforms. The force also finally began to find a role within the military as a guerrilla and auxiliary force to supplement the Army in the event of invasion. The Home Guard began to prepare for any possible form of enemy attack. In the photo below men from the 3rd Liverpool Battalion can be seen demonstrating tank destroying skills to men from the Cheshire Home Guard. The Liverpool men had apparently built the dummy tank themselves and used it in numerous exercises.

The Home Guard were in fact quite adept at adapting everyday objects for their new role. An old bottle, rag and some petrol became a tank-busting Molotov Cocktail for example. Some units even managed to adapt ordinary cars by adding thin sheets of metal to create an armoured car.

Other units would use less orthodox methods of transport such as push bikes due to the petrol shortages. The photo above demonstrates how times had changed, showing an example of Local Defence Volunteers in civilian clothes on the right facing Home Guard in uniform on the left.

In addition to its duties during an invasion members of the Home Guard often involved themselves in other activities such as fire watching, guarding bombed out sites and patrolling sensitive areas such as docks or factories. This was usually in addition to a normal daytime job meaning many had to survive on very little sleep! Some anti-aircraft defences were also manned by Home Guard units, releasing regular army personnel for duty elsewhere.

From its informal and amateur beginnings the Home Guard grew into a well trained force that undertook many of the normal duties the Army performed, even going through assault courses such as the one on the left. As the war went on and the tide turned in favour of Britain and her allies an invasion became less likely. Over time the role of the Home Guard had to be redefined to meet new challenges. As is mentioned on page 76 they were stood down in December 1944 and disbanded a year later.

Business District

ANY CITY that thrives on commerce and trade requires a business district, an area of offices, banks, insurance companies and exchanges. In 1940s Liverpool these mostly had their premises in the streets around the Town Hall, some of which are believed to have been laid out at the time Liverpool was granted its first charter. In addition to these firms there were also prominent local government buildings such as the Municipal Annexe, the Coroners' and Magistrates' Offices, Exchange Flags and the city's main Post Office.

Clearly any damage caused in this area would have a knock on effect on the city's response to the bombings. Bombs falling on a viaduct on the approaches to Exchange Station isolated it for three months, passengers having to get off a stop early and switch to alternative means of transport. When the Post Office was burnt out business had to move to the Fruit Exchange on Victoria Street whilst repairs to the lower floors got underway. Imagine arriving for work one morning to discover your workplace has been destroyed like the Corn Exchange below!

Apart from being the home of prominent businesses the buildings in this area had great architectural beauty and significance. The Town Hall for example is the city centre's second oldest building dating back to 1754. It is still possible today to take a walk through the area and be amazed simply by looking up at the upper floors of buildings, beyond the drab commercial frontages and bright signs of the ground level. Most of these older photos are easy to place despite post war construction work, due to the image containing a distinctive building.

This photograph features the Government Buildings which once stood on the corner of Victoria Street and Sir Thomas Street. During the war the building housed the Ministries of Health and Agriculture, the Unemployment Assistance Board and the Office for Inland Revenue. The building was hit by a high explosive bomb on the night of 3rd/4th May 1941 which penetrated the upper floors of the building and buried two firewatchers who were in the basement of the building waiting until incendiaries fell in the area. A third watcher called Ernest Leatham managed to work his way free and obtain the help of Constable William Hunter in freeing one of the other men, but the second was difficult to rescue. Leatham, a employee of the Ministry of Health remained at the site removing valuable papers and re-assuring the trapped man. This rescue took over 7 hours to complete during which time Leatham and his fellow rescuers were in grave danger from the falling masonry and fires all around them. Leatham and Hunter were later awarded the British Empire Medal in recognition of their work that night.

The site has never been built on and is currently used as a pay and display car park. The balustrade that once surrounded the building remains to remind people of what once stood here. The site is perhaps one of the last remaining large bomb sites in the city centre. On the left can be seen the tower of the Municipal Annexe.

Liverpool's Head Post Office was located in Victoria Street between Stanley and Sir Thomas Streets. Already damaged during raids in March 1941 the building was hit by incendiaries shortly before 11pm on 3rd May 1941. More followed shortly before midnight and despite the best efforts of the fire-watchers, Home Guard, the Auxiliary Fire Service and the Fire Brigade it was all the men could do to slow the fire enough to allow important documents and post to be removed. Around 4am the steel girders in the ceiling collapsed and although some fire-fighters stayed until the next day the building was almost completely burnt out. Work moved to the Fruit Exchange whilst the lower floors were repaired.

Thanks to the men's efforts the building was saved and soon back in use although the top floor was later removed. The building remained in use as a post office until being recently converted into an indoor shopping centre known as the Metquarter which opened in March 2006.

This view along Victoria Street from opposite Temple Court shows another aspect of the Head Post Office building. It dates from September 1941; four months after the building had been gutted and rendered unusable. Scaffolding on the building shows that extensive repair work was being undertaken at this time. This reflects the importance of the building to the city's communications since skilled workers and materials were in very short supply. The docks and railways understandably took priority and many buildings remained in a poor state until the late 1940s or early 1950s. The phone box on the right has white corners to make it more visible during the blackout. Behind it stands the Commercial Saleroom Building, which stored and sold fruit.

As has been mentioned the Post Office lost a floor but has recently been converted into the Metquarter shopping centre. It was workers from this building that were responsible for repairing the communication lines with Western Approaches which is discussed on page 61. The former saleroom on the right has some very interesting iron work on the balconies and in an entrance arch facing Temple Court. It is currently occupied by a firm of solicitors. The tram lines that once ran down the centre of the street became redundant soon after the last tram service was cancelled in 1956. Buses have taken over now but Victoria Street remains an important part of many routes.

The second building on the right is the Head Post Office which we have seen on earlier pages. This photo was taken before the night of 3rd/4th May as the Post Office was badly burnt out that night and New York Buildings were also hit.

Stanley Street has retained most of its old buildings, the only major change to this half is the Head Post Office being converted into the Metquarter shopping area. The large modern frontage of this can be seen on the right having replaced New York Buildings. This half of Stanley Street is closed off to most traffic, the

This shows the view up Stanley Street from Whitechapel. The closest buildings on either side were named after American cities, Chicago on the left and New York on the right. This reflects the close ties between the USA and Liverpool which became especially close during the war. Not only were many Americans based in the region but the vast majority of those serving in Europe passed through the city.

exception being the taxi rank. The area remains popular with Beatles' fans eager to see the sights of Matthew Street (where the Cavern Club once stood) which is on the left a short distance down Stanley Street. Opposite Matthew Street is a seated statue of Eleanor Rigby by the local Sculptor Tommy Steele. Recalling a line from the Beatles' song of that name it is dedicated to "all the lonely people".

photograph was taken shortly after the raid on 3rd/4th May 1941 when this damage was done. Under the rubble in the foreground was buried a policeman named Frederick Doran. A native of Ireland he joined the Liverpool City Police after World War one and had twice been rewarded for helping stop runaway horses on the streets of the city. He was last seen by another policeman in Williamson Square in the early hours of that night. Despite the best efforts of the people seen here his body was not recovered until the 8th May 1941. At the same time were also recovered another policeman called George Shellshear and two civilians, Walter Ellery and William Jones.

This photograph shows the corner of Whitechapel and Sir Thomas Street. On the right are the remains of the Shakespeare Hotel and behind it (on the corner of Whitechapel and Stanley Street) would have stood New York Buildings. The presence of such a large number of rescue workers suggests that this

The tram lines visible in the wartime image have long since been removed and this part of Whitechapel is now pedestrianised. After the war the area once occupied by the Shakespeare Hotel and New York Buildings was cleared. A post office and truck yard for the same was built here. These have recently been cleared away to make way for the Metquarter development.

The photograph on the right features the offices of the Liverpool, London and Globe Insurance Company Ltd on the corner of Dale Street and High Street. On the night of 6th/7th May 1941 the building was hit by a high explosive bomb which shattered all the windows. The Town Hall, which stands on the other side of High Street just to the left, was also hit and the Council Chamber became temporarily unusable.

The damage caused during the May Blitz was so bad that by the morning of the 7th May none of the roads between Tithebarn Street and Dale Street were free to traffic. An emergency water pipe runs across High Street with sandbags there as a temporary measure to allow vehicles to use the street.

Since the war the building has been taken over by a branch of the Royal Bank of Scotland. The building has recently undergone external repairs giving it a quite different aspect to the darker soot-blackened building of 1941.

This photograph shows the junction of Castle Street on the left with Dale Street on the right and Water Street straight ahead. Early on in the war it became common practice to try and protect buildings with the use of sandbags and this can be seen here on both the Town Hall (right) and the Martins Bank Building. Sand was also used extensively to fight the fires started by incendiary bombs. During the dark days of May 1940 the vaults of the Martins Bank Building were temporarily used to store a large part of the nation's gold reserve prior to it being shipped to Canada. Although sworn to secrecy and told only that they would be receiving "boxes of unknown content" many of those involved knew only too well what was being transported and were relieved when the consignment left the port intact.

This view has changed very little in the intervening years, the main exception being the loss of the tram

system. It's interesting to note the much darker exteriors of the buildings in the wartime image. Years of soot and pollution had given the city's buildings a rather dirty appearance. Recently many of them have been cleaned with varying levels of success. Martins Bank merged with Barclays in 1969 and they currently occupy the building. The Town Hall, which was built in 1754 has played host to visiting royalty and famous stars such as the Beatles who would acknowledge the crowd from the balcony seen here.

This photograph shows employees of the Corn Exchange outside their workplace sometime after it had been reduced to rubble during the night of the 2nd/3rd May 1941. In the background on the right can be seen the corner of India Buildings, itself lightly damaged during the bombing raids. The latter was an important building containing a post office, numerous consulates and the offices of a number of shipping lines such as Holt and Blue Funnel. On the far side of the building from this was an entrance to James Street Station from which a subway ran to the main platforms below James Street. Also worthy of note is the bicycle in the foreground on the right. With the introduction of petrol rationing this form of

transport became increasingly popular for short distance journeys. Wartime caption writers would have made much of the fact that these employees continued to turn up for work and do business in the streets, refusing (as did so many others) to be cowed by the Luftwaffe and doing what they could to keep the war effort going.

As has been mentioned elsewhere the Corn Exchange building was rebuilt after the war. The damage to India Buildings was also repaired allowing visitors and locals alike to marvel at its sumptuous interior. Cars have ousted bicycles in this picture but many commuters still rely on public transport due to the high costs associated with city centre parking.

Cook Street runs from Castle Street to North John Street. On the left once stood the Cook Street arcades which contained a number of small business premises until it was demolished by enemy action in 1941. The site of the arcades was later cleared completely and the basement was used as an emergency reservoir of water to help combat future raids. On the right is a branch of the Bank of England and in the distance are some of the elegant buildings on Castle Street.

During the war petrol was rationed, so people had to resort to alternatives such as steam or gas. A steam traction engine can be seen in the photograph on the right, assisting with clearance work on the arcades. This photo shows the reverse view down Cook Street to that above right.

The site of the arcades was used as a car park for a time before being replaced by a plain modern building in the late 1950s that looks quite out of place with its surroundings. The city is fortunate that so many buildings on Castle Street such as the former

Adelphi Bank (the right hand building in the distance) survived the war intact.

This photograph shows damage inflicted on the premises of the Peerless Refining Company. This firm refined fats such as margarine and lard. Both of these were used extensively during the war as a substitute for butter and lard was used in the production of soap. This versatility made firms such as Peerless important parts of the war economy, and their loss would have been keenly felt. Shortages of soap, combined with people being made homeless in the bombing meant that mobile bathing units, originally designed for troops at the front were used on the home front. The main entrance of Peerless was on Cheapside but this view shows the rear of their building from Cunliffe Street. The factory, offices and warehouse were destroyed by fire on the night of 3rd/4th May 1941. The heat was so intense that palm oil ran down to Dale Street, eventually congealing into a deep mess. Over 400 tonnes of the company's stocks of margarine and lard were lost that night. Not far away in the area between Marybone and Vauxhall Road the firms of Calthrops, Atlas and Central Oil also suffered badly, mainly through hits from HE

bombs. One such bomb struck a gas main, setting it alight and leaving a jet of flame 20 feet into the air. Thousands of tonnes of animal feed, oils and raw materials were lost and all three firms had buildings either destroyed completely or burnt out.

The modern site of Peerless Refining is now occupied by offices and apartments. Only the building on the far left remains unchanged.

This view shows the junction of Vauxhall Road on the right, Tithebarn Street straight ahead, Hatton Garden on the left and behind the cameraman would be Great Crosshall Street. The tall building in the middle of the photo was the City School of Commerce, and just to the left of this stands the "Rising Sun" public house. The building on the left was a newsagents, and a variety of shops. A bank and two pubs once occupied the area on the right. Part of the façade of Exchange Station can just be seen in the distance.

Although the road layout has remained much the same most of the buildings have now been replaced. Exchange Station closed in the 1970s but fortunately the façade was retained when the site was converted into a modern office block known as Mercury Court. Both the City of Commerce building and the Rising Sun pub have survived, although the former is now privately owned offices. The building on the left is a modern housing development which has a newsagent on the ground floor. The tall modern building on the right is an example of the kind of student accommodation which is very common in this part of the city now. A modern symbol of Liverpool, the superlambanana stands outside.

This photo was probably taken at around the same time as the last one and shows the view down Tithebarn Street towards the junction on the previous page. The Walker's pub on the left is the Rising Sun, the City School of Commerce is mostly hidden behind it. The remains of the building to the right of this jutting out further into the street would have been the St Nicholas Church Institute. On the right would have stood the warehouses of McFie and sons, a sugar refining firm. Sugar was an important part of Liverpool's history, and firms such as Tate and Sons (later Tate and Lyle) were major employers, producing around 550,000 tons per annum in the early 1970s. When the Tate and Lyle factory was demolished a decade later it brought an end to 300 years of sugar refining in the city.

As was mentioned on the previous page much of the area has changed but the two buildings on the left remain.

The Church Institute was demolished after the war with a modern extension to the School of Commerce replacing it. The modern housing development mentioned in the previous page has replaced the warehouses and includes a car park on the ground floor. More examples of modern student accommodation can be seen in the distance, a reflection of the city's highly successful universities.

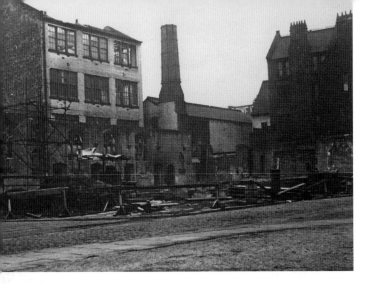

The Catholic church of St Mary stood on the corner of Highfield Street and Cockspur Street. The building was designed by Augustus Welby Pugin, who also designed the original St Oswald's church in Old Swan along with a Convent of Mercy and Orphanage for the city. The building was originally erected in 1845 on Edmund Street but was taken down piece by piece and rebuilt here ten years later. The original site was needed for the expansion of the nearby Exchange Station, the approach lines for which ran very close to this new site. St Mary's was not the first Catholic church on this site. Worship here can be traced back to the early eighteenth century when the first Roman Catholic church in Liverpool since the reformation was built here. At the time it was built this site was on the edge of the city. Its isolation and uniqueness made it an easy target for anti-Catholic rioting that followed events like the Jacobite uprising of 1745. This was when the Catholic Bonnie Prince Charlie invaded England trying to regain the British throne for the house of Stuart. On the night of 3rd/4th May 1941 this building was all but destroyed leaving just the shell shown here.

After the war the building was rebuilt in a modern style which opened in 1953. This modern church closed in 2001 and was demolished in 2003. The site is earmarked for development into flats. The Northern Line still runs close to this site but now goes underground to Moorefields Station as Exchange Station was closed in the 1970s.

This photo shows the view along Vauxhall Road looking towards the junction on page 47. The large building on the left is the North Dispensary, which provided medicine for the area including the David Lewis Hospital which stood a short distance away in Leeds Street. Contemporary newspaper reports often showed pictures of bomb damaged hospitals alongside outraged headlines which spoke of barbarity and "terrorist raids". A number of hospitals or similar buildings suffered damage in the raids, the most notable of which was Mill Road Infirmary where around 60 people died as a result of a parachute mine landing there. In the distance can just be made out the spire of the Municipal Annexe buildings on Dale Street.

Since the war much of this area has changed including some roads disappearing, but since the dispensary stood roughly opposite Philips Street taking a comparison is relatively easy. The Dispensary is no longer standing; in its place are modern business premises and a car park. The only recognisable survivor in the modern image is the spire of the Municipal Annexe which still pokes up above the modern buildings in the distance. Just behind from where this photo was taken stands a memorial to over 70 people who lost their lives in the Blackstock Gardens Shelter when it was hit on the 21st December 1940.

Holy Cross church once stood at the junction of Great Crosshall Street and Standish Street. Designed by Edward Pugin it was opened in 1860. Even though this wartime photograph appeared in the *Daily Sketch* for September 17th 1941 no raids occurred on that day. The church was probably another casualty of the night of 3rd/4th May 1941. Also hit that night was Holy Cross School in Addison Street and its attached shelter killing many people sheltering there.

The church was rebuilt after the war, reopening in 1954. The restructuring of inner city parishes meant closure in 2001 and the building was recently demolished to make way for modern housing. Nearby is a small garden containing a war memorial to the men of the church who fell during World War One (below).

This now includes tablets in memory of the church and people who died in the war.

Funding the War

FIGHTING WORLD War Two was a costly affair for Britain, as the country spent heavily on the equipment and raw materials this required. The government however was not the only source of money for waging the war, private citizens and organisations were encouraged to raise funds through a variety of themes. In addition to directly helping fund the war effort many activities were launched to promote local events or relief efforts.

All people were enlisted in this activity as youngsters were encouraged to turn in their treasured collections of shrapnel and bomb casings in order that the metal could be recycled.

These could range from the ironic use of an unexploded bomb to store donated change (bottom right) which raised over £50, to events that required more organisation such as the touring of downed German warplanes. Top right can be seen a Junkers 88 bomber being towed through the city accompanied by students. It is believed that this may be the same plane that was shot down at Bromborough Pool on the 8th October 1940. People were no doubt reassured to see that although the heart of the city was being torn out, the raiders were vulnerable to the city's defences.

Nor was it only bombers that the public could see. Below can be seen a Messerschmitt 109 fighter plane on display near St George's Hall. It is unlikely that this plane was shot down nearby since its limited range would not permit it to reach the region.

One of the larger types of funding people could provide was through the National Savings Certificates system. The authorities would work out how much was required to purchase a Spitfire for example and then challenge a town or city to buy one of their own. The public often got into the spirit of the occasion, especially students. For one week in October 1940 a group of engineering students tried to persuade people to buy War Bonds by dressing up, one man as Hitler, and the other as a hangman as can be seen right. The local papers reported that "Hitler's" neck was hardly out of the noose all day!

Regular formal presentations helped to promote Liverpool's financial contribution to the war effort, making locals, the press and government aware that the city was giving its all in Britain's darkest hour.

Derby Square to Church Street

THIS STRETCH of the city centre and the roads running from it comprised a major part of Liverpool's shopping district. Some firms like Bunneys and Coopers were locally known, others such as Woolworths, Marks and Spencer and C&A were familiar to any traveller. Tram routes such as the 8 and 33 also passed along these roads on their way towards the city's southern suburbs. The nature of trams meant that any fallen rubble on the route had the potential to block the whole route at that point, forcing services to terminate and start outside the city centre. This meant that rubble from demolished buildings was often put back on the site of the building until it could be removed at a later date.

The fact that the area suffered terribly is attested to by the panorama view above. Taken from somewhere near the current Trials Hotel it shows the ruined area of Lord Street, South Castle Street and beyond. Despite the immense damage however there were many surviving buildings, a will to turn misfortune into opportunity and a determination not be beaten. Some of the basements of demolished buildings became storage places for water known as Emergency Water Supplies in preparation for future attacks.

The city was determined that no more buildings would be lost for a lack of water to fight fires that broke out during raids.

The area has seen a great deal of change since the war with the construction of shopping centres such as the Cavern Walks and Liverpool One or buildings such as the Queen Elizabeth Law Courts. Whilst the architecture is often a poor substitute for the Victorian and Edwardian splendour they have replaced, these new shops hopefully represent a brighter future for the city.

This photograph shows the view along Harrington Street from Castle Street. On the left stands the premises of W. Barratt and Co boot manufacturers, a company that survives today under just the surname. On the right would have been part of the St George's Crescent buildings. Shoe and boot making was a reserved occupation during the war, preventing or limiting such skilled tradesmen from joining the armed forces. This helped to ensure that the armed forces were supplied with footwear, even though that meant shoes and other clothing being rationed for civilians. Although rationing was often unpopular and even circumvented by people with enough money to buy from the black market it did at least ensure that most people received a reasonable share. Post-war shortages and the need to feed a recently liberated Europe meant that rationing did not finally come to an end in the UK until 1954. Despite its suffering and economic troubles after the war Liverpool was in the forefront of raising money for charities seeking to "Save Europe from Famine". Meetings attended by the Bishop of Liverpool and local MPs were held in Picton Hall to publicise the problem.

Although the Barratt's building survived the war intact it was later demolished to make way for this modern replacement which now houses the offices of a recruitment agency. On the right can be seen the corner of Pearl Assurance House, seen on the left on page 59.

This photograph was taken from Redcross Street across towards James Street on the left and Derby Square on the right with Fenwick Street in the centre. In the foreground the outline of the buildings that would have been on Preeson's Row can be seen, the site fenced off for safety. The row consisted of the usual mix of merchants, and ship brokers with the Queen's Hotel at the far end. This whole area was pelted with incendiaries and high explosive bombs during the night of 3rd/4th May. The Victoria Monument, like St Paul's Cathedral in London stands out, unscathed in an area devastated by the bombing raids. This photograph was obviously taken sometime after the 3rd May since work is well underway to clear the rubble and the roads have all been cleared. Visible in the background are India Buildings, the National Bank, the North and South Wales Bank, the Midland Bank and the Victoria Monument.

Although Redcross Street still exists it is now mostly used for access to a car park.

Preeson's Row has been replaced by a series of modern buildings including a modern public house on the site of the Queen's Hotel. This photograph was taken from a little to the right of the original due to the presence of the new buildings on the left which would otherwise have blocked most of the view. The Victoria Monument still survives and the surrounding Derby Square is currently undergoing a facelift.

This photograph has appeared in a number of books but proved elusive to place, despite the tower on the left which appeared to belong to a church. The photo was taken from Derby Square looking towards South John Street. The building with the tower was known as Church House and was home to numerous Church of England societies including a number dedicated to overseeing the construction of the Anglican Cathedral. The building was also home to business premises on the ground floor such as Werner's, a firm of tailors. The building in the background on the right was a branch of Martins Bank. In the foreground members of the Women's Royal Voluntary Services provide a much needed tea break for the men labouring to make the area safe.

The modern comparison has been taken from further back than its wartime equivalent as the presence of new buildings prevents an exact comparison and blocks the view towards South John Street.

This view shows the St George's Crescent and Derby Square area from Castle Street, a part of the city badly hit during the war. The "specks" in the upper half of the photograph are not marks on the negative but part of the tram system's power lines, the number giving some idea of just how important this junction was to the city. What seems like a square tower on the far right of the photo are in fact the remains of the Custom House dome which was damaged more than once during the blitz. Behind the tram on the left can be seen the kind of fencing often erected after raids to prevent access to bombed sites. These were frequently painted white to help drivers to see them during blackouts. The tram on the right behind the group of people is coming up South Castle Street.

After the war much of the area behind the fencing was grassed over and used for parking. The buildings that survived the war on South Castle Street were demolished in the mid 1970s and the area eventually made way for the Queen Elizabeth Law Courts which is the brown building in the background on the right.

It was in this area that the Liverpool's castle stood, although its remains were demolished in the eighteenth century. The square building on the left was erected on the site of St George's Crescent but failed to retain the shape that gave this area its name. South Castle Street has vanished completely.

This photograph shows the other side of St George's Crescent on the left and some buildings in Lord Street on the right. The sign above the damaged building refers to Austin Reed, a tailors. St George's Crescent was laid out as early as 1829 by John Foster Senior but as has been seen all of the buildings on both sides were lost during the war. In the foreground an ARP warden surveys the destruction.

The modern view is taken from a slightly different angle to give a better view of the modern buildings that have replaced Foster's work.

This is the view along South John Street from near the junction with the now defunct Atherton Street. The damaged building on the left was the main telephone exchange which in fact controlled three exchanges.

The building was hit by incendiaries on the night of 3rd/4th May 1941 and despite the best efforts of the firewatchers and night staff the building was soon burning out of control and had to be abandoned. Fortunately most of the equipment was salvaged which allowed the easy transfer of services to temporary buildings until a more permanent home was set up in Seel Street. Assisting in these repairs were staff from the Head Post Office who managed to restore full communication to the nearby Western Approaches in just four days. This was a vital operation since Western Approaches was the nerve centre of the Battle of the Atlantic. It also allowed the staff there to plot the downfall of the German battleship *Bismarck* just over three weeks later. In the distance can be seen the dome of the former Royal Insurance Building on the corner of Dale Street and North John Street.

As with much of this part of Liverpool the whole of South John Street is now part of the Liverpool One shopping centre which has changed it beyond recognition. This view is taken from the upper level to ensure the buildings on North John Street can be seen, giving the reader a point of reference despite the great changes that have taken place.

Located at the corner of South John Street and Atherton Street the Custom House Hotel was named after the magnificent classical building just a short distance away. During the war the area was heavily bombed and the hotel was hit on 11th October 1940 destroying the interior and leaving just the outer wall seen here.

After the war the area was cleared and left landscaped until recent times. Atherton Street no longer exists making a precise comparison impossible, but South John Street remains as part of Liverpool One. This comparison was taken from the lower level of the shopping centre.

Woodhouse's furniture store on Lord Street stood a short distance down from South John Street. On the 4th May 1941 nearby fires in Cable Street threatened the rear of the building. Staff had hung the windows there with carpets as a blast precaution and attempted to keep these safe by constantly spraying them with water. By 7am however this had failed and the building was abandoned. The building was burnt out but as most of the others on this side were hit by high explosive bombs Woodhouse's was one of the few buildings on this side still standing. In the foreground of this shot runs an emergency water main.

Although the building was patched up and survived the war this side of Lord Street was later rebuilt in a much more modern style. The building on the right is on the corner of South John Street and is part of the Liverpool One shopping centre.

here to remove some of the rubble from the demolished buildings. Before the war the buildings that were once here would have contained a music dealers, the Liverpool School of Music, a branch of the Kodak Company and numerous outfitting firms. On the right the burnt out shell of Woodhouse's furniture store can just be seen. The extensive damage to this area resulted in numerous panoramic photographs showing the extent of the devastation. Sadly most of these were taken from either an upper floor or roof of nearby buildings making a modern comparison difficult.

This view shows the corner of Paradise Street on the left and Lord Street on the right and demonstrates the extensive damage that this part of the city suffered. This view is clearly taken during the winter months as snow lies on the ground and on the roofs of some of the vehicles present. The lorries would be

Like the rest of Lord Street this section was rebuilt after the war along the same frontage in the rather drab style so common to the post war period. Most of the streets in this area are now pedestrianised, a far cry from times when they would be filled with carriages, vehicles and trams. The buildings on the left form part of the recently completed Liverpool One project.

This photograph shows the view along Paradise Street to its crossroads with Lord Street, Whitechapel and Church Street. Many premises on both sides of the street have been totally destroyed. On the right at Number 29 until 1937 would have stood the Museum of Anatomy. This contained quite a few unusual specimens that were sold to Louis Tussaud's waxworks in Blackpool. On the left at Number 28 once stood the offices of Condensed Milk Producers Ltd. This form of milk retained much of its nutritional value but was able to be stored without refrigeration in cans for years. During wartime, with few houses owning fridges this became quite important. The lamposts have been painted with a white band to make them easier to see in the blackout. The tower of the Municipal Annexe can again be seen poking up above some of the few buildings to survive on Lord Street.

The modern viewpoint shows drastic change, most of which has come in the last few years. Paradise Street itself was closed for many months as the Liverpool One project was being built, and its various shops now line both sides of the now pedestrianised street. In the distance on the right are some of the few surviving buildings including the Beehive public house and the former Coopers department store, now a branch of Vera Moda, a clothing store.

This photo was taken in Basnett Street looking across Church Street. The presence of the hoses and rubble in the foreground suggests this was taken shortly after the attack and shows that the buildings were badly gutted by high explosive bombs and fire.

A quick check on the buildings in this photo confirms how important a shopping area Church Street has been. The building on the left was once the department store George Henry Lee's but is now occupied by a clothing store. Opposite is now the Primark store, but the building was originally built in the early 1950s for Littlewoods. To the right covered in scaffolding stands Marks and Spencers.

This photograph shows the other side of the buildings featured on the previous page and was clearly taken immediately after the raid as fire-fighters are still working to put out fires within the smouldering shell. The premises on the near corner of the building were occupied by Russell's Ltd, a watch and jewellery merchants.

The Littlewoods Building, now occupied by Primark is officially known as Spinney House. Its style is very decorative for the post-war period including sea nymphs and anchors and reminds some of India Buildings on Water Street. This leads many people to mistakenly believe it was built during the 1930s whereas it was in fact finished in 1955.

This photograph shows Parker Street which runs from Clayton Square to Church Street. At the start of the war the building on the left with the clock was occupied by a travel agents whilst next door was an opticians.

Although many of the buildings in this area were cleared to make way for the Clayton Square shopping development both the buildings on the left survived, although the clock has long since gone. Both Parker Street and Church Street have been pedestrianised.

This photo shows Church Street from its junction with Clayton Lane, looking towards Lord Street. It was clearly taken sometime after those on pages 66 and 67 since the façade of Robinson and Cleaver and the bookshop has been demolished and the area cleared. Beyond this was Burtons, Woolworths and at the end with the square tower stood Coopers department store. The nearest shop on the right performed electrolysis treatment. Beyond this but mostly out of shot was Broadbridge's Opticians and on the other side of Parker Street Bon Marche department store. The twin towers of Compton House are easy to make out next. Although once a hotel the building was occupied by Marks and Spencers at the time of this photograph. Two trams can be seen in the distance as can the junction with Whitechapel, Lord Street and Paradise Street, sometimes known as Holy Corner.

Burtons remain but Woolworths later moved to the St John's Shopping Centre before closing recently when the company went into receivership. Marks and Spencer still occupy Compton House and the building is currently undergoing renovation work.

The Littlewoods building was constructed in the 1950s in a decorative style reminiscent of pre-war architecture. The YMCA building has since been demolished. The whole of Church Street and most of the streets running off it are now pedestrianised areas.

The Bluecoat Chambers in School Lane is the city centre's oldest building dating back to 1718. Originally the home of a charity school, the building later became an arts centre. On the night of 3rd/4th May 1941 incendiaries started fires in the area. Due to a lack of water the entire east wing (seen here on the right hand side of the photograph) and the upper floors of the centre block were gutted. Fortunately for the city all the artwork stored in the building had been moved to the ground floor of the central block and so were saved by the efforts of the building's firefighters.

On the next night though the rear wing was

destroyed by a high explosive bomb. Some idea of the extent of the damage can be gauged from the photograph on the right which shows the remains of the concert hall shortly after the attack.

The building was rebuilt in the same style, work finishing in the early 1950s making it difficult to believe from a glance at the exterior that the building was so badly damaged. It's interesting to note that the trees have also survived although they're now considerably bigger! The Bluecoat has recently re-opened having undergone a refurbishment allowing it to play host once more to art galleries, shops, a café and a bar.

Lime Street and Ropewalks Area

THE STREETS in this part of the city represent the other half of the shopping district. From department stores like Lewis's and Blacklers to market stalls within the St John's Market Hall you could find a shop here to suit your tastes and budget.

The area was more than just shops however, Lime Street alone containing 3 cinemas, numerous pubs and one major hotel, not to mention the superb St George's Hall and the mainline train station. St George's Hall can be seen in the photograph above. In the foreground can be seen the monument to the King's Regiment or "Kingos". One of the oldest infantry regiments in the army with origins going back to 1685 it was associated exclusively with the city from 1881 before merging with the Manchesters in 1958. The monument is a timely reminder that Liverpool people not only fought and died in their home city, but also on active service in Europe and Asia.

As with many areas looked at in this book the story is a mixed one. Many buildings were lost or suffered serious damage but many others survived with little more than broken windows, a dangerous fire hazard but comparatively fortunate. The city owes a great deal to those civilians who volunteered for dangerous duties such as fire watching – spending the night in a building keeping watch for incendiaries in order to put them out as soon as they landed. Newspaper articles from the war reported allegations that a lack of firewatchers led to buildings such as the Central Library and Rotunda Theatre being lost. It's quite possible that these reports were permitted because it may have encouraged more volunteers to come forward.

Both train stations in this area, Central and Lime Street suffered damage during the war and the resulting cut in communications impacted on both morale and recovery for a few days until the damage could be repaired. Apart from the impact on the locals the difficulty in travelling into the city from outlying regions meant that rumours about heavy casual-

ties, martial law and people calling for surrender were rife amongst nearby towns. Although untrue these got as far as being repeated in German propaganda broadcasts.

A psychiatric report quoted in the *Liverpool Post* for 5th March 1941 suggested that the psychological impact of the raids on the civilian population was minimal, and what impact there had been was on civil defence and armament workers who lacked sleep. Although this report probably glossed over some genuinely serious cases local civilians remained defiant as the image above right shows. Typical Liverpool humour was also present. One hairdresser whose shop suffered damage put up a sign declaring

"We've had a close shave. Come in and get one yourself!"

Post war recovery and modern development has seen significant changes in the area but many of these views are still recognisable. Many damaged buildings were either repaired or simply rebuilt by the company in a more frugal style, reflecting the post war economic struggles. Fortunately the kind of wholesale demolition necessary to achieve designs like those below never came to pass. Put forward in February 1943 the design would have seen the loss of such gems as the North Western Hotel, the Empire Theatre and the Dr Duncans pub and completely changed the face of the area.

the exception of James Wilson the men were all members of the Air Raid Precaution Rescue Service, once again demonstrating the dangers inherent in the role. During the war there was an ARP post located in London Road which perhaps explains why so many of them were killed in one night.

Thomas J. Hughes founded his business in a shop in London Road with just £150 and 3 staff. The company are still based in London Road although they now have more than 50 stores

This photograph shows damage to the pavement in front of one of T. J. Hughes' stores in London Road. This occurred during the night of 21st/22nd September 1940. Although it might seem relatively minor in comparison to some of the other photographs in this book in reality at least 3 people are listed as having keen killed at the store that night, Agnes Wilson, James Wilson and Thomas Bradley. Elsewhere in London Road five other people were killed, Mary Beswick, Frederick Jowett, Sarah Maylor, Sarah McDonough and James Reedy. With nationwide and employ around 3,000 staff. Then as now the company occupied three different premises in London Road making it difficult to determine where the original photograph was taken. This modern photograph shows the largest of their three stores. The area in the foreground is known as Monument Place due to the presence of an equestrian statue of George III located close by. The statue was originally intended for a site in Great George Square but this location was eventually chosen as it was on the main coach route into the city.

This image shows the extensive damage that the William Brown Library suffered during the air raids. It shows the rear of the building and was taken from the now vanished Clayton Street. The first line of defence for the buildings on William Brown Street was 8 night watchmen backed by 11 volunteer firewatchers who would usually be drawn from staff members. On the night of 3rd/4th May 1941 a HE bomb landed close to the Walker Art Gallery shattering most of the glass there. Shortly after fire bombs landed on the nearby museums but were put out before they could do too much damage. Just after midnight a larger HE bomb fell on the library trapping three of those present and starting a major fire. All three were later rescued and the fire gradually brought under control. Later that night more HEs fell near to the museums doing further damage there. Although this photograph dates from 1955 it clearly shows that the building was extensively damaged for reasons outlined on the next page.

After the war the area to the rear of the buildings on William Brown Street was changed forever by the construction of a series of flyovers and roads which make a direct comparison impossible. The library and museum were rebuilt after the war and although their frontage looks very similar the rear and interior for both was considerably altered. The library is currently closed whilst it undergoes major building work. In the background can be seen the unique St John's Beacon

This view up William Brown Street shows the Library, and Picton Reading Rooms on the left and the Wellington Column on the right. A number of street shelters can also be seen. Although not obvious in this photograph most of the buildings on this side of William Brown Street suffered heavy damage. Some 185,000 books were lost in the library along with countless exhibits in the nearby museum. The national press, noting that most of the damage was caused by fires blamed a lack of firewatchers. In reality the staff present had done the best they could and had at least successfully contained the fires until the arrival of an AFS pump which succeeded in putting the fires out temporarily. By morning the all clear was sounded, but soon after a change in wind direction saw sparks from other nearby fires spread to the library through the ventilation shafts. Some of these went down the ventilation shafts into the basement. From there fires once again caught hold and quickly spread to both the museum and Technical College doing considerable damage to both. When these were

finally put out staff entered the flooded basement to find floating in the water Audubon's *Bird's of America* a priceless work which proved only slightly water damaged. It has recently gone back on display.

This modern comparison was taken from slightly further back as otherwise the trees that were planted in the area would block the view of the Wellington Monument. William Brown Street is no longer open to through traffic. It is mostly used for taxis and the pavement has also been widened.

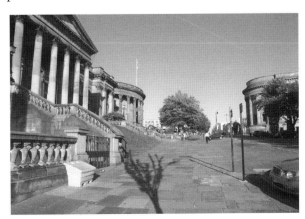

Although not showing any damage to buildings this photo is of interest for showing the local Home Guard marching past St George's Hall on Lime Street. This was their final parade before standing down in 1944. These men would shortly pass by on their left the Cenotaph, a memorial originally dedicated to those who fell in what was then called the "Great War". Shortly after this photograph was taken the dates 1939-45 would be added to those of 1914-18 and the "Great War" became known as World War One. It's quite possible that some people in this parade had seen service in both conflicts! The buildings in the centre background of the photo contained a number of hotels including the Imperial Hotel which displayed large neon signs advertising Guinness, Martell Brandy and Schweppes. Behind these buildings stood the old St John's Market.

This area saw extensive change after the war and none of the buildings in the background of the earlier photo survive. St John's Beacon and the St George's Hotel (now part of the Holiday Inn chain) mark the location of the modern St John's Shopping Centre. The large screen in the centre of the photo is the modern day replacement for the neon signs and shields a rather ugly modern car park from view. St John's Market, rebuilt in a modern style is still on the same site.

The statue on the right (whose legs can just be seen in the wartime photo) is of Queen Victoria's consort, Prince Albert.

The steps of St George's Hall (known as St George's Plateau) have long been the focus of mass meetings. Sometimes that will be in sorrow such as in the aftermath of John Lennon's death or in protest such as during the 1911 Transport Strike, or even in celebration such as this photograph from VE day. The sea of people is clearly in the mood to rejoice, with one brave woman even perched on the top of a lampost! In the centre of the picture is the cenotaph which provides a poignant reminder that many of the people in this photograph will be living with the sorrow of dead family members, whether they be from the armed forces or civilians. Running down Lime Street seems to be a series of flags, possibly those of the victorious Allied nations.

Today's Plateau is much quieter although much of the view remains the same today. The tall building on the left is the former North Western Hotel which dates to 1871. This magnificent building was saved from potential demolition and converted into student accommodation. To the right of this is the entrance to Lime Street Station the frontage of which is currently undergoing a facelift. To the right of this can just be seen the Crown Hotel. The equestrian statue is of Queen Victoria's consort, Prince Albert and behind the statue is the former Forum Cinema. In the place of the tram now stand buses that use this part of Lime Street to reach Queen's Square bus station. The Cenotaph still remains the focal point for the city's memorial services.

This photograph shows the view from St George's Plateau towards Islington. Although taken in 1948 it demonstrates how even older buildings such as St George's Hall were adapted during wartime as the low brick structure to the left of the nearest car was the entrance to an air raid shelter. The hall was slightly damaged during the war and also used for war work such as the issuing of ration books. In the background from left to right are the Walker Art Gallery, County Sessions House and the buildings on Commutation Row. The column is topped by a statue of the Duke of Wellington. Erected in 1863 rumour has it that the metal used to cast the statue was taken from cannons captured at the Battle of Waterloo. Although the war was over by the time of this photograph the presence of relatively few cars can be explained partly by the fact that petrol rationing only came to an end in 1950.

The modern day comparison shows a slightly wider view to give a good idea of what buildings now stand here. The business premises that once stood on Commutation Row have been replaced by one large building containing apartments and offices. The shelter entrance has since been removed. The statue on the right is of Queen Victoria and behind it stands the Empire Theatre. St George's Hall has seen something of a revival recently, re-opening to regular visitors in 2007, just in time to be a central part of the Capital of Culture opening ceremony. The building and its surrounding area forms part of Liverpool's World Heritage Site.

Roe Street once ran from St John's Lane to Hood Street, passing the Royal Court Theatre and Queen's Square along the way. This photograph shows the fire engine from Durning Road which fell afoul of a crater in the middle of the street on the night of 21st/22nd December 1940. This night was particularly busy and the raid was the longest launched against the city to that date. A large number of incendiaries were dropped and many landed in this area setting fire to

St George's Hall and the Fish Market which once stood on Great Charlotte Street. The situation was bad enough that fire brigade reinforcements were called for from the surrounding areas, something that would become increasingly common as the attacks continued. Some indication of the hazards of driving in a blacked-out city during an air raid can be gauged from the fact that the local crew failed to spot this crater in time and sadly all 7 members died in the resulting crash. Although the machine would eventually be extricated from the crater and possibly even repaired the loss of such trained personnel would have been a major blow for the city.

After the war Queen's Square became a bus station known as the Gyratory. This in turn was replaced by the station seen here, known by the name of the square. Roe Street runs to the right of the pedestrian crossing and Hood Street to the left. Much of the area around the station was redeveloped around the same time. None of the buildings seen in the original photograph survived the post war development of the area.

This photograph shows two cinemas that used to occupy neighbouring buildings in Lime Street. On the left was the Futurist (1912) and on the right was the Scala (1916). Originally opened by independent owners they came under the same management in 1920. The Futurist was the first purpose-built cinema in the whole city and both were early pioneers in the city of "talkies". Prior to this films would be accompanied by music played by an organist or even an orchestra within the cinema. At the outbreak of war cinemas were initially closed for safety purposes but soon re-opened when their morale boosting effect was understood. Through newsreels they provided a visual method of keeping people in touch with events, and through movies they helped to entertain people. In this photo it can be seen that both were damaged during the war, the Futurist being put out of commission for a month and the Scala for 6 weeks.

The post war decades have not been kind to cinemas and declining attendances have seen most close down. The Scala closed in 1982 and has since been used as a licensed bar, nightclub and restaurant before its current incarnation as a lap-dancing club. The Futurist also closed in 1982 but since then the building has remained empty. Although both retain much the same external appearance they have suffered a sad fate considering they played such an important role in our local heritage.

This view shows two of the city's finer buildings, the Lewis's department store on the right and the Adelphi Hotel on the left. On the night of the 3rd/4th May 1941 a high explosive bomb hit Lewis's, ironically knocking out the sprinkler system. Incendiaries and more high explosives followed and soon the building was ablaze. Sparks and burning debris soon fell on the nearby Blacklers store (see page 83) setting that store alight. Despite the best attempts of fire fighters a water failure in the area doomed the building leaving it nothing more than a gutted shell. The Adelphi suffered shattered windows and some damage to one wing. A booklet given to American soldiers serving in the UK listed the Adelphi as one of the city's largest hotels and as also having one of its best restaurants. With such an endorsement it's no surprise that many servicemen could be seen at the hotel during the war.

Although patched up the original store was never quite the same and in the 1950s a new building was constructed on the same site. Sadly after several years of financial problems the store closed on the 29th May 2010 after 153 years in business. The Adelphi is still open for business and remains one of the better known hotels in the city. The booklet mentioned earlier informed the servicemen that "shops are not open on Sundays", a practice that is no longer adhered to by most shops.

This view of Lewis's Department store shows just how extensive the damage was and why it was necessary to partially demolish the building shortly after the raid. By mid July this had been accomplished and the area to the right of this photograph was safe enough that the Fairclough Street entrance to Central Station was back in use. The demolition work was completed shortly after the war in preparation for the new building, the third incarnation of this famous department store on this site.

A section to the left of this photograph survived intact due largely to the fact that lifts and stairwells separated it from the remainder of the building. The post-war building retained the size of its predecessor but lost much of its decorative style. The statue above the main entrance is affectionately known locally as "Dickie Lewis" but its official title is "Liverpool Resurgent" and was sculpted by Jacob Epstein. It was unveiled in 1956 and caused both amusement and controversy at the time as the naked figure was considered too anatomically correct in certain areas!

opposite side of Great Charlotte Street and also gives a clear view of the extensive damage.

After the war the company built a new building in the same style on the site and remained in business until it closed in 1988. The building is now occupied by smaller businesses including restaurants, banks and one large pub named the Richard John Blackler in honour of the founder of the department store. Due to the addition of new buildings opposite the McDonalds a direct comparison was impossible but this view shows the same side of the store. In the distance on the left can be seen the hotel above the St John's Shopping Centre.

In Great Charlotte Street stood Blacklers, another department store. This building was hit by burning debris and sparks on the same night as Lewis's, some of the latter coming from that store. It also fell victim to the mains failure in the area that night which left a shortage of available water to fight the fire effectively. The interior of the store and all its goods were destroyed, although the shell survived. The store was forced to move temporarily to a number of shops on nearby Bold Street in order to continue business. This second photo, right, shows the view from the

At the corner of Colquitt Street (right) and Wood Street once stood the firm of Brown Brothers, a motor and cycle accessories firm. By the time this photograph was taken their premises had been utterly wiped out along with the Grapes public house which would have stood a little further up Wood Street. The building on the right was part of the former St Luke's School which in May 1941 was being used to temporarily store mail. On the other side of the school stood a new telephone exchange, a vital communi-

cation link. Fires started here on the night of 5th/6th May 1941 endangered both the school and exchange but were eventually put out by the hard work of an AFS crew from Lytham St Anne's. The tower in the centre is a ventilation shaft for Central Station and the unfinished tower of the Anglican Cathedral can just be seen in the background.

Modern office premises have replaced both the bomb site and St Luke's School, blocking the view towards the Anglican Cathedral.

of the church from being destroyed. The sound of the church's bell crashing to the ground from the tower was heard some distance away.

Unlike St Nicholas' (see page 24) which was rebuilt St Luke's stood derelict for many years after the war before being dedicated as a memorial to those who were killed during the Blitz. Recently the interior has been used by local art groups to hold exhibitions and concerts. The same group has also been recording the wartime experiences of locals. This particular photo shows artwork from Yoko Ono. Although the interior was cleared up and the internal pillars removed poignant reminders of the damage such as burnt timbers at the base of the tower remain. In the area behind the camera some of the church's stained glass windows survive, an example of which is shown above right. In the grounds of the church is a memorial to the victims of the Irish Potato Famine of the 1840s as many of its survivors moved to the city.

Designed by John Foster Senior in 1811 and completed by his son by 1831 St Luke's church stands on a prominent site at the corner of Berry Street and Leece Street. On 5th May 1941 an incendiary bomb hit the church starting a series of fires. As this was the height of the May Blitz the emergency services were already stretched and were unable to prevent the body

This photograph shows the view down Seel Street towards Hanover Street in the distance and Concert Street behind the photographer on the right. The large gap on the left hand side of the street was part of the premises of Goodlass, Wall & Co who made colours and varnishes (see page 88). The first building on the right was the premises of Collinsons' boot manufacturers. The next building along was owned by the British Glass Co Ltd and a sign advertising "glass" can just be seen. With so many shattered windows around the city during the air raids it's not difficult to imagine how busy this firm and others like it would have been during and after the war!

The lost buildings on the left were never replaced after the war, but the nearest has been converted into a car park. The side wall of the building next door has another piece of painted artwork on it. In that block of buildings are a café and the Liverpool Academy for the Arts. The latter was established as recently as 1988 but built on the legacy of men like William Roscoe the abolitionist MP for Liverpool in the late eighteenth century. The former premises of Goodlass, Wall & Co are currently undergoing building work and are surrounded by scaffolding. What had been the British Glass Company is now one of the city's nightclubs, many of which are situated in this area. The buildings of the recently completed Liverpool One shopping area can be seen in the background.

Probably named after the royal family on the throne when it was laid out Hanover Street was once a very fashionable residential area of the city during the eighteenth century. By wartime however it had largely been taken over by business premises. This photograph shows the view towards Ranelagh Street in the distance. Seel Street is in the foreground on the right and College Lane is opposite it. On the fateful night of 3rd/4th May this area was hit badly by a mix of high explosive and incendiary bombs. A shortage of available water nearby caused the employment of hose tenders to bring water from further afield and no doubt hampered efforts here. Amongst the premises damaged that night were Tyrer's Wine Distillery and Elam's, a firm of stationers. A factory belonging to Littlewoods that made parachutes was also hit. Fortunately the night shift that would normally have been present had been sent home but three of the firewatchers present died that night.

Hanover Street is still dominated by business premises although many of these have seen a revamp in recent years with the completion of the Liverpool One project. Part of this will stretch across Hanover

Street to the site on the corner of Seel Street which can be seen behind the hoardings on the right. Although this looks unchanged from the wartime image the land was in fact built on after the war but the premises have since been demolished. Just beyond that site is the Hanover Hotel, one of the few pre-war buildings on this stretch of the street still standing.

This photograph shows the view from College Lane, past its junction with Hanover Street and on up Seel Street. Most of the roads running off Hanover Street parallel to Seel Street form what are known as the "Ropewalks" area of the city. Large quantities of rope were vital to a sailing ship, so as the port grew Liverpool quickly developed a thriving rope-making industry centred on this area. This required a narrow, straight and long stretch of open ground in order to lay out the fibres that would be twisted together to form rope. As the city expanded the industry gradually moved further away and the area was quickly laid out into streets, often named after local merchants who had their house nearby. Sadly, like Hanover Street, Seel Street also suffered its fair share of damage. The firm of Goodlass, Wall & Co, whose paint factory was located between Seel Street and Wolstenholme Square was hit on the nights of 21st/22nd December 1940 and 3rd/4th May 1941 doing extensive damage on both occasions. No doubt the highly flammable paint added to each night's conflagration making the work of

the firewatchers and fire-fighters much harder. It was for similar reasons that imported stocks of timber and wood were usually moved away from the docks as soon as possible.

Since the war the area has undergone extensive redevelopment and regeneration. The main similarity between the two images is the layout of the roads as few if any of the buildings in the wartime image survive, and the streets are no longer cobbled.

The Attackers

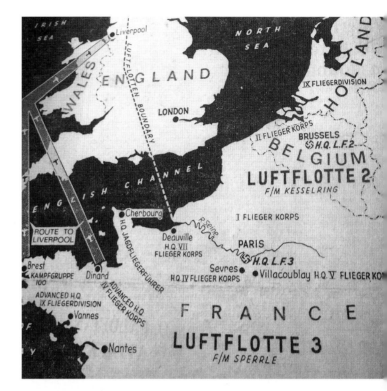

THIS IS Field Marshal Hugo Sperrle, commander of the Third Air Fleet during much of the period that Liverpool was under attack. He was a skilled veteran of the First World War who had commanded the Condor Legion (German volunteers fighting for Franco's nationalists) during the Spanish Civil War. It was planes under his command that were responsible for the bombing of Guernica in 1937. From their bases in Northern France his squadrons saw action in bombing raids against many British industrial cities including Birmingham, Plymouth and Liverpool. Their route to Liverpool is shown above right, taking them over Cornwall and Wales rather than a straight line so to avoid unnecessary contact with the British night fighter squadrons and anti aircraft concentrations

Sperrle's squadrons were mostly based in North Western France having moved there after the fall of that country in June 1940. They generally employed night raids against Liverpool since daytime raids had proven very costly for them. The main German fighter at this stage of the war, the Me109 simply did not have the range to help support the bombers for long which left them vulnerable.

After the war Sperrle was put on trial as part of a group of high ranking German military personnel, charged with war crimes, crimes against peace and crimes against humanity. Sperrle was one of only two in the group who was acquitted on all counts and lived until 1953. Despite the claims in the press men like Sperrle were no more intentionally targeting civilians than their RAF equivalents.

The Germans were never able to attack the city with impunity and on occasion a plane would be shot down but not destroyed. One such plane, a Junkers 88 (shown below left) crash landed at Bromborough Dock around 4pm on 8th October 1940. It had been shot down by three Hurricane fighters flown by Czechoslovakian pilots based in Speke. The crew were quickly disarmed by a local man named Harry Gill and taken into custody by a military unit stationed nearby. The observer had been killed by the machine gun fire of the fighters and two other crewmembers were badly hurt in the crash landing.

The bomber contained a new type of bombsight which was captured intact and studied by the authorities. According to Harry Gill there was also an extensive map of Liverpool and its surrounding area inside the cockpit. The plane belonged to Kampfgruppe (Battle Group) 806, primarily a reconnaissance unit. Despite its parent formation's usual role the plane was still carrying live bombs when it crashed. A captured JU88 bomber in flight is shown above.

The corpse of the observer, Lieutenant Herbert Schlegel was buried with full honours in Hooton village church where they remained until 1962 when the remains were transferred to a German military cemetery in Staffordshire. The temporary grave can be seen below right.

In addition to the Junkers 88s of Kampfgruppe (Battle Group) 806 two other Luftwaffe formations saw extensive action against Liverpool. Kampfge-schwader (Battle Wing) 55 mostly operated Heinkel HE111s and flew from bases in Northern France. Their symbol, seen on the left caused some con-fusion, with some believing that it was some sort of red dragon similar to that seen on the Welsh flag. In reality it was another mythological creature, the half eagle, half lion creature known as a griffin.

A typical HE111 can be seen top. As most of the raids against Liverpool tended to be at night the German planes had to be guided to their targets to ensure any degree of accuracy. The responsibility for this generally fell to the pathfinders of Kampfgruppe

100, who were based in Vannes in Brittany. Their symbol was one of the Norman ships from the Bayeux Tapestry seen above right. They also flew Heinkel HE111s but these were often specially modified to enable the use of special radio signals to guide them to their target.

Although the Germans already had extremely accurate intelligence maps of the city (often based on Ordnance Survey maps) these were of little use at night. Once in the area they would then mark the target with flares for the following planes to improve their accuracy. Later on British scientists managed to learn how to jam these signals and reduce the enemy's accuracy.

Internees

DURING THE war the government were seriously concerned that "enemy aliens" (people born in a country the UK was at war with such as Germany or Italy) would present a serious problem to national security and a total of around 27,000 of them were interned in camps. One of these camps was set up on a newly completed housing estate in Huyton. The estate was surrounded with barbed wire and guarded by the military but internees were able to organise concerts and Christmas parties. The picture above shows a round-up taking place with internees, carrying some meagre belongings being marched under guard to a train station. All German, Italian and Austrian males aged between 16 and 60 were initially rounded up but the majority were soon released. Some of those interned included people who had fled from the persecution of the Nazis.

For the remainder they lived an isolated existence on estates like the one at Huyton seen on the right. Some were not quite as fortunate as it was initially the policy of the government to use mainland camps as a temporary measure whilst internees were being shipped to camps on the Isle of Man. This stopped after the SS *Arandora Star* carrying more than 1,200 internees and a small number of prisoners of war to Canada was sunk by a U-Boat on the 2nd July 1940. A total of 805 people drowned, 713 of them German or Italian and the remainder either crew or military guards.

The policy of internment on mainland Britain however continued until 1942 when most of the camps were closed down. Huyton's camp was based around the Bluebell Estate.

Dissent and Spying

THE SPIRIT of the British people during wartime was remarkable, and Liverpool people in particular dealt with the horrors of bombing and the struggles of rationing particularly well. It should never be imagined however that there was not dissention and disagreement in the region about the various wartime policies of the government or local officials.

Disenchantment with the authorities took many forms and even began before the war. Writing in the *Liverpolitan* in January 1938 George Thompson decried the poor preparations being made to defend against air raids, pointing out that although many people had been enrolled in roles such as auxiliary fire fighting and gas detection they still awaited equipment and training after many months.

It is worth noting that he was writing 22 months before war broke out and more than two years before the first air raids over Merseyside. This concern reflected a very real fear that was expressed by Stanley Baldwin when he stated that "the bomber will always get through". People really did believe that without an adequate series of precautionary measures the Luftwaffe would reduce British cities to dust.

George Thompson wrote a number of articles during that period criticising what he saw as the poor preparations and whilst many of the faults he highlighted would have been resolved before war broke out some remained. The press cited the lack of trained firewatchers as one of the major causes for the loss of buildings such as the Central Library. Recruiting firewatchers and fire-fighters was no easy task however as many people were already working long weeks and doing additional voluntary duties.

There was considerable opposition to using women firewatchers and firefighters, especially in the latter role. Attempts to make it compulsory for women to undertake fire watching duties in their street or place of work were opposed locally and provoked great debate. The objections ranged from reasonable to bizarre, with one Alderman suggesting that women would have their night's sleep disturbed by the hundreds of rats that infest docks and warehouses at night, implying that men would somehow sleep like a baby!

This debate was taking place in late 1942 which we now know is after the final raid on the city. It is interesting to see however that even 5 years after George Thompson first highlighted them, some issues were still outstanding.

The coming of war did create an atmosphere of co-operation and a sense of everyone being in it together, but did not eliminate disagreement entirely. Early on in the war posters urged people to write to their MPs objecting to the bombing of Germany in case it provoked retaliatory attacks against British cities. It also accused what it called "bloodthirsty old men", especially those with wealth of seeking to provoke slaughter which would fall primarily on working people rather than the rich. These efforts were of course in vain as soon both Britain and Germany would be engaging in regular air attacks on each other.

Other people attempted to work against the government line during the war. In early 1940 the Duke of Bedford attempted to facilitate peace with Germany through a friend who had contacts at the German Embassy in Dublin. The Duke, was a patron of the British People's Party, a far right organisation which favoured an immediate end to the war. The moves that the Duke made came to nothing but he was eager to ensure that his position was understood and arranged meetings around the country to explain the "truth" behind them. One of these was held in Picton Hall, Liverpool on the 4th April 1940.

Another pre-war problem was that many were paranoid about Germans living in the UK and what plans they may be making for the day war came. When circulars calling for a unification of Germans abroad for social purposes (alleged to have come from the German Consulate) the *Liverpolitan* was deeply sceptical. It pointed out that the German Consulate had recently been alleged in court to have arranged contact between the employee of a munitions firm and the German secret service. The man supposedly stole official plans of the factory and sold them on for a handsome sum. This atmosphere of mistrust and allegation no doubt influenced the British government decision to intern enemy aliens when war broke out (see page 92).

During wartime the public were constantly reminded through posters such as "Careless Talk Costs Lives" and "Keep Mum, she's not so dumb" that a casual conversation could be easily overheard by enemy agents. In reality the Germans had a poor success rate when it came to infiltrating Britain. The close knit communities that existed in most of the country made strangers stand out easily and many spies were "turned" and used to give false information. Through spies the Germans did learn some local information though. The infamous Lord Haw Haw (real name William Joyce) once referred to people on Scotland Road hanging out white flags after bombing raids in one of his broadcasts from Germany. It is thought that this was prompted by the sight of white curtains billowing through bomb-shattered windows.

Docks

AS HAS been seen already Liverpool's docks were crucial to Britain's fight for survival and the Allied war effort, making them the prime target for the Luftwaffe's bombers. This also made them a high priority for repairs in order to maintain a regular flow of troops, food and materials. In almost every family there would be a member either at sea or in an occupation linked to it, either directly such as dockers, or indirectly such as insurance agents and carpenters. Some of the docks were also used as a home for Royal Naval vessels.

Most of the docks were named after famous local people, for example Gladstone Dock is named after William Gladstone, the only person to become Prime Minister of Great Britain four times. He was born in Rodney Street in 1809. It was in the docks that one of the most infamous incidents of the war occurred – the destruction of the SS *Malakand* in Huskisson Branch 2 Dock. Although this is discussed in more detail on page 104, the after shot above and the before shot below give some indication of the force of the explosion.

Damaged sheds at South Canada 3.

Despite the best attempts of the Luftwaffe to destroy the port the dock system stood up remarkably well. Sheds had been gutted, machinery damaged, quays covered in rubble and even ships sunk in some docks, but for the most part this was temporary. Immediately before the May Blitz the weekly tonnage return was 181,562, immediately after the weekly figure dropped to only 35,026. Thanks to the hard work and Herculean efforts of the dock board and Liverpool people this figure rose to 85,678 tons the next week and by mid June was virtually back to normal. The result of this hard work can be seen in the photograph on the left which shows an American truck being unloaded at one of Liverpool's docks.

Unfortunately many of the dock images are difficult to take comparisons of due to the area normally being out of bounds. In view of this I have included on these pages some images without a modern equivalent in order to give an impression of the scale of the damage.

SS Silvio *sunk in Alexandra Dock 1.*

Damaged sheds and crane at South Gladstone Dock 1.

The sloop HMS Wild Goose *receives a warm welcome as it enters Gladstone Dock in February 1944.*

Today many of Liverpool's docks are no longer used for cargo shipping. Those that are in use are not always easy to gain access to, making comparison photography difficult but often rewarding. Just imagine the response you would get had you told a docker in 1941 that the warehouse he was standing next to would become a series of luxury flats like the one below (Waterloo Warehouse) in just over half a century!

Located just a short distance to the south of the Pierhead, Wapping Dock suffered damage more than once during the war. This view shows the warehouse buildings that stood adjacent to the Dock Road and Overhead Railway. The centre section of the warehouse had been hit in September 1940 but was patched up and put back into use. This was made easier by the fact that the building was divided into 5 separate fireproof sections. On the night of 2nd/3rd May however a parachute mine landed in the area causing extensive damage. The Overhead Railway was especially vulnerable and hits to it could also impact on the dock railway systems that ran below.

Although the current warehouse building looks largely the same it is in fact shorter than its pre-war counterpart. The first section from the clock end back to the repaired section in the wartime photograph was demolished after the war although some of the columns remain. On the left the dock pump house which controlled the dock gates and the gate keeper's lodge have both survived. The warehouse has been converted into luxury flats and modern buildings now line the far side of the dock. The Overhead Railway closed in 1956 when high maintenance costs and a fall in passengers saw the company go into voluntary receivership. Despite vigorous public campaigning it was removed the year after allowing the road to be widened.

Opened in 1846 by Queen Victoria's consort Prince Albert the Albert Dock was considered very modern for its time. It utilised a hydraulic cargo handling system for the enclosed dock with its extensive quayside warehouses. After just 20 years however the rise of larger steam powered cargo ships saw the dock fall out of favour since the entrance and basin were too small to cope with the increase. Trade fell until by 1920 virtually no ships visited and the warehouses were being used to store goods for transport by other means such as rail or road. It was given a new lease of life during WW2 when it was used by both Merchant and Royal Navy vessels and the dock suffered some damage during the war that can be seen still present in the Chambre Hardman photograph from 1947 on the right.

After the war the dock was once again redundant and when the whole dock system fell into decline in the 1970s Albert Dock was no different. Pictures from this period show a silted up dock, ruined warehouses and somewhat surprisingly the WW2 damage still present! Fortunately in the early 1980s the Merseyside Development Corporation set to work restoring the dock and warehouse complex. The site now contains the Merseyside Maritime Museum, the Tate Art Gallery, the International Slavery Museum and numerous shops, cafés, bars and restaurants. As part of this regeneration the damage was finally repaired and the dock dredged making it possible for ships to return for events such as the Tall Ships.

©NT/E.Chambré Hardman Collection

This image shows in more detail the damage inflicted on this part of the Albert Dock which remained without repair for over 30 years.

The city is fortunate to retain the Albert Dock as we see it now, since prior to the Merseyside Development Corporation stepping in the alternative plans included massive office blocks involving the demolition of all of the warehouses, or the dock being filled in to create a series of offices around a central plaza.

An important part of the Liverpool docks system was the Princes Dock and nearby landing stage. The dock was designed for sailing vessels trading with America but by the turn of the twentieth century the dock was concentrating on Irish trade and the landing stage on the large transatlantic passenger ships from firms such as Cunard and White Star. From 1895 passengers destined for those liners could travel by rail to Riverside Station which stood between the dock and river. During the war many of those same liners were converted to troop ship service and transported hundreds of thousands of troops to the city. Both the landing stage and station played their part, allowing those troops to be transported quickly and easily from the liners onto the mainline railway system. In this photograph some of the thunderbolts seen on page 18 are seen being unloaded onto the landing stage and in the background is one of the liners.

After the war the rise of air travel saw a sharp drop in demand for transatlantic liners and the landing stage was all but demolished in the mid 1970s. Riverside Station closed in 1971 and was demolished in the 1990s, the site now being occupied by office blocks. In recent years the Cruise Terminal has been built close to the site of the original landing stage but is not usually open to the public making a direct comparison difficult. This one was taken from the pavement overlooking where the stage would have been. This area also occasionally plays host to visiting Royal Navy ships including HMS *Ark Royal* which was built on the Mersey at Cammel Laird's Shipyards in Birkenhead.

Opened in 1856 the Stanley Dock is one of the few docks in Liverpool on the landward side of the Dock Road. Originally the dock was flanked by two warehouses like this but towards the end of the nineteenth century part of the dock was filled in and the vast Tobacco Warehouse (which stands opposite this one) was built in 1900. The 14 storey Tobacco Warehouse was used throughout the war as a storage depot for American forces and was even visited by Eleanor Roosevelt,

wife of the wartime US president. The warehouse is so big that it was possible to drive her around it in a jeep! This photo from 1942 shows one of the original warehouses and the damage that had been inflicted on it earlier in the war. This photo was deemed worthy of censorship with the top half of it to be shaded out, presumably so that people wouldn't see the damage.

After the war Stanley Dock remained in use until the 1980s when, like the rest of the dock system it became largely redundant. The damage inflicted on it

during the war was never repaired and that section was demolished to be replaced with modern buildings. Although the Tobacco Warehouse currently houses a heritage market each Sunday neither of the original warehouses are in use. Sadly although these buildings are works of art and a shame to see in such a condition they are difficult to put to modern use. It is hoped however that a new canal link between the dock and the pier head might bring renewed interest in this area.

This photograph shows just a small section of the massive Stanley Dock Tobacco Warehouse. As mentioned on the previous page the building was used by the US Army as a storage depot for much of the war with dockers working under the supervision of US Army officers and personnel. One of these can be seen on the right of this photograph in a greatcoat and cap. The barges seen in the foreground would still have been an important form of transport in wartime, especially here as the Stanley Dock connected to the Leeds Liverpool Canal. The canal itself suffered heavy damage on the night of 20th December 1940 when a delayed action bomb burst on the canal's banks not far from here between Bankhall Bridge and Athol Street. The canal was breached and water flooded into a nearby railway yard. The resultant loss of water hindered efforts to fight the fires which raged in the nearby docks and timber yards. After the damage had been repaired sections of the canal were reinforced with extra planks to reduce the amount of water lost if there was another breach. The overall canal also formed part of a defensive stop line with sections being reinforced with pillboxes to help slow down any enemy moving inland from the Lancashire coast.

Although now used by canal boats passing through to the Pierhead the dock is still relatively quiet. This particular warehouse survived the war without any serious damage and remains in use today as the location of the Heritage Market.

The SS *Malakand* was berthed in Huskisson Branch Dock Number 2, loaded with ammunition and explosives. At around 11pm on the 3rd May 1941 a barrage balloon came down on the ship, closely followed by a series of incendiaries which set light to the balloon.

Even though these fires were put out fires from the nearby sheds spread to the ship and made it untenable, forcing the crew to abandon her. Although both the crew and local fire-fighters fought a hard battle against the fires from the dockside the ship exploded at 7:30am the next day scattering debris throughout the area and devastating the dock. This can be seen in this photograph above which was taken from the Overhead Railway on the Dock Road. The official death toll for the explosion was given at 4 but the incident was played down and the likely figure is closer to 20 or 30. As a direct consequence of the event instructions were issued that in future ships would maintain the minimum crew and auxiliary steam to move their vessel away from the quay if it became necessary.

After the incident Huskisson Branch Dock Number 2 was filled in and is now used as a storage area. The dock sheds on either side belong to Huskisson Branch Dock 1 (left) and Huskisson Branch Dock 3 (right). As the Overhead Railway is no longer in existence this comparison was taken from ground level to the left of where the original photograph was taken.

This view shows another damaged section of the Overhead Railway, this time by Canada Dock Station. The dock opened in 1859 and mostly dealt with timber, primarily from the country it was named after. During the war large warehouses were set up further inland to reduce the time the highly flammable timber spent in the vulnerable dockside area. Like its neighbour Huskisson Dock, the quayside sheds were badly damaged. The Overhead at this point had already been damaged in December 1940 when two spans were brought down by a direct hit. This view shows fires still burning in the dock and hoses crossing the Dock Road, drawing water from the dock for use on fires inland.

Although Canada has three branches and a graving dock a quick study of where Canada Dock Station once stood helps to locate the correct modern view. The removal of the Overhead Railway once again results in a much wider Dock Road, although on most weekends traffic here is limited. In addition to the

Overhead Station there was also a mainline station and a number of goods warehouses nearby but these are either closed or demolished now. In the '50s and '60s the dock became a dock for cargo liner firms such as the Harrison line but today it is mostly used as a scrap metal depot and for bulk cargoes such as oil.

Convoys

AS A densely populated island with extensive colonial possessions Britain relied heavily on trade for food and essential supplies in order to carry on the war, trade carried on merchant ships to ports like Liverpool.

In peacetime these would sail alone but during wartime this would make them easy prey for enemy submarines as there would not be sufficient naval escorts to protect each ship. By sailing in a convoy of several merchant ships the Royal Navy stood a much better chance of being able to protect them as it could concentrate several anti-submarine ships against any attack. One of these convoys can be seen above at sea.

Liverpool's connection to these convoys was not just as a point of departure or arrival. As has been mentioned elsewhere in the book the Battle of the

Atlantic was managed from 1941 onwards from Western Approaches headquarters, based in Derby House. The staff there had responsibility for an area of the Atlantic that covered the approaches to all the ports on the western side of Britain including Liverpool, Bristol and Plymouth.

The headquarters were staffed by women from the Women's Royal Naval Service and the Women's Auxillary Air Force alongside personnel from all branches of the armed forces. Their role was to work together to co-ordinate convoys and their defence.

The convoy system was used extensively throughout the war with considerable success. Each convoy typically had between 30 and 70 ships in it, and some idea of how efficient the city's docks were can be gauged by the fact that an average of 4 convoys passed through the system every week!

Famous Visitors

AN IMPORTANT part of maintaining civilian morale was the impression that the authorities, both local and national cared about the plight of the people on the receiving end of the air attacks. This was often demonstrated by visiting the area and offering words of condolence to victims and encouragement to the population. Sometimes the visits would be combined with fact finding missions such as speaking with local industrialists, at others the civil defence units would be reviewed and given a chance to demonstrate their skills.

Sometimes the visits would appear unannounced with only a few in senior positions being forewarned in order to make the advanced arrangements, but often local people found out through unofficial sources. Both the Prime Minister and Royal Family always received a warm welcome from the city and were cheered by people in the streets. The King and Queen felt they had shared some of the people's hardships as Buckingham Palace had been bombed 7 times during the war, including once when the family were in residence. They can be seen visiting one of the city's block of flats in the photograph below.

The Prime Minister Winston Churchill visited the city on a number of occasions and took care to visit the docks and speak to workers there. He considered the Battle of the Atlantic to be of paramount importance, once stating that the U-Boat peril was the one thing that scared him during the whole war. He was well aware that the fight against the U-Boats was only half the struggle: to keep the country fed and the war effort going he knew it was essential to keep ports such as Liverpool open.

It was visits such as these that helped to counter the feeling that the city was being ignored in favour of targets such as London or Coventry.

In the photo below right he can be seen being driven down Lime Street, saluting the crowds who have turned out to greet him. A study of the buildings in the background shows the Vines Public House and the Scala and Futurist Cinemas, allowing us to make a modern comparison (below).

In addition to royalty and the Prime Minister the city was also visited by foreign dignitaries. A female sniper from the Soviet Union visited the city in 1942 as part of the Soviet Officers' Delegation. Their role was to promote links between the two countries and also inspect the British war effort to see if there was anything they could learn from it. This was of course a far cry from the reception any similar delegation would have received a few short years later with the outbreak of the Cold War!

The heads of many governments in exile were based in Britain, sheltered by the country whilst their own was occupied by Nazi Germany or her allies. Some of these visited the city including the Prince and Princess of the Netherlands and the King of Norway. In addition the wife of the American President, Eleanor Roosevelt also came to inspect US troops as is mentioned on page 102.

Across Merseyside

ALTHOUGH LIVERPOOL'S docks were the main target of the German raids the whole Merseyside region also suffered, and not by accident either. Bootle to the north along with Birkenhead and Wallasey across the River Mersey contained extensive dock systems of their own that were equally important for dealing with convoys and as berths for Royal Navy vessels.

Like Liverpool the raids on the rest of Merseyside tended to come in fits and starts. For Wallasey the worst months were December 1940, with 121 fatalities coming in just three days and March 1941 with 189 casualties. Many buildings were heavily damaged during the war including the Town Hall in King Street which is pictured right after a raid in August 1940. In total some 332 people were killed and 286 seriously wounded in the borough by the raids.

In Birkenhead the major raids occurred in December 1940 when 63 people died and March 1941 when 228 died. Once again many famous buildings were hit including the Argyle Theatre in Argyle Street (a photo of its badly damaged interior is top right), the Laird Street bus depot and Birkenhead Park Station.

Birkenhead suffered 382 deaths and over 600 serious injuries as a result of the raids. In Bebington the damage was somewhat less with around 60 fatalities.

One area particularly badly hit though was Bootle which suffered more than 400 fatalities and over 200 serious injuries in raids that devastated the borough, damaging or destroying some 85% of the houses in Bootle and leaving perhaps as many as 25,000 people homeless in the May Blitz alone. Alongside these important buildings such as the County Hall, Johnson's Dye Works and Marsh Lane train station were also damaged.

The story of the rest of Merseyside's experience of the war is not confined purely to the suffering under air raids however. The region's industries were turned over the war production, with Lever's in Port Sunlight assembling over 1,400 Jeeps and military vehicles and Cammell Laird turning out both naval vessels and merchant ships. The Liverpool-based firm of Littlewoods also had factories in the Wirral which were turned over to producing barrage balloons and parachutes.

Just as in Liverpool the people of the surrounding boroughs volunteered in large numbers to help the war effort and to limit the impact of the raids. Their hard work and courage was recognised at the time by the award of a large number of medals for bravery. There were also numerous visits to Bootle and the Wirral by Winston Churchill and the Royal Family who always received a warm welcome. The King and Queen were even able to walk down the centre of a recently bombed street in Wallasey without fear of being harmed as can be seen on the left.

Overall the war provided the people with Merseyside with a shared experience that crossed the boundaries. Bootle may have been a separate borough and Wirral in a different county but everyone shared the pain, suffering and loss of loved ones that the air raids caused. The war united people as very little else could, and when the news that Germany and then Japan had surrendered was announced people across the region celebrated as never before, relieved to have survived such momentous events.

South of the City Centre

THIS SECTION will deal with the area that includes the outskirts of the city such as area around the cathedrals and universities and the outlying suburbs such as Toxteth and Wavertree. The area has a great deal of variety, containing slums equal to anything off Scotland Road but also large mansions and areas of parkland. The photograph on the right appeared in the *Liverpool Post* for 21st September 1940 and shows a mansion's "palm house ballroom and grotto" that had been hit during a recent raid. Some of the districts like Toxteth have been settled as far back as the Vikings if not earlier, others such as Wavertree Garden Village were only built up in the twentieth century.

As I mentioned in the introduction to the book the city is more than just its prominent buildings, and any story of the Liverpool Blitz should include as much detail as possible about the people who lived through such a traumatic period. Where known I have tried to include the details of any casualties or dates. Where this was impossible I have included some related information about the city's experience.

As many houses were rebuilt after the war, often in the same style as those around them the people who currently own the house will often have no idea that their home was once the scene of either death or a lucky near miss.

Known as the Mount Pleasant Presbyterian Church this building stood on the corner of Mount Pleasant and Great Orford Street. It was built in 1827 for a congregation who originally consisted of Scottish immigrants. By 1877 it had become part of the Presbyterian Church of England but the church was closed in 1939 when the congregation merged with Trinity Church in Princes Road. In the background of this shot would once have stood the Liverpool Workhouse, one of the largest in the country, sometimes housing as many as 5,000 people. The workhouse site was purchased in 1930 for the purpose of building a Catholic cathedral.

The famous architect Edwin Lutyens drew up the first design for the site but these had to be scaled back after the war. Adrian Scott (brother of Giles who designed the Anglican Cathedral) was commissioned to do this but his designs met with criticism and never went ahead. The current cathedral, the tower of which can be seen in the background was designed and built in the 1960s after Sir Frederick Gibberd won the design competition. The design incorporates Lutyens' crypts, the only part of his design to be completed. After the war the site of the Presbyterian church was sold to the cathedral and this building, the Liverpool Science Park was recently constructed here.

This wartime image shows a part of Brownlow Hill close to the junction with Pembroke Street. The photograph is dated 22nd September 1942 but the damage would have occurred sometime before this as there were no raids on the city that month. In the background on the left can be seen the tower of Victoria Buildings, part of the University of Liverpool. On the right can be seen one of the surviving buildings of the Liverpool Workhouse. Often thought of as Victorian institutions this particular one had its origins in the 1730s and had stood on this site since the 1770s. A product of the Poor Laws they were intended as a place where poor people could live and work. In reality many were poorly run and a place of desperation for those who wound up there. Families who entered were quickly separated as men and women had separate wards. Liverpool's included its own chapel and conditions were generally considered better than average. The lamp on the building on the left is likely part of the Dragon public house.

The modern day photograph was taken from slightly further back at the junction with Great Newton Street as Pembroke Street no longer connects with Brownlow Hill. The site of the buildings on the left has now been replaced with a modern university building. Victoria Buildings, which were built in 1892 have survived and are now open to the public as a gallery and museum. On the right can be seen part of the Catholic Cathedral, including the crypts mentioned on the previous page.

The church of St Catherine was consecrated in 1831 and dominated the eastern side of Abercromby Square. Like the Custom House on page 28 it was designed by John Foster Senior and consisted of a large neoclassical design. On the night of 6th/7th May 1941 the building was burnt out by fire, the results of which can be seen here. A working party is busy in the remains of the building but only the outer shell and the classical façade survived the war. The blaze here was so fierce that the nearby Oxford Street Heart Hospital had to be evacuated in case it spread. It was eventually brought under control by pumps from Durning Road Fire Station along with reinforcements brought in from as far afield as Newton-Le-Willows and London.

Declining post-war attendances meant that re-opening St Catherine's was impractical. In 1952 St Catherine's parish was merged with St Stephen the Martyr's on Grove Street. After the war the property in Abercromby Square was gradually bought by Liverpool University for housing its various departments. The shell of St Catherine's church was no exception and although it remained until 1966 it was eventually demolished to make way for the modern building seen below which is known as Senate House. Fortunately in recent years the universities have tended to refurbish and preserve existing older buildings, saving such gems as the North Western Hotel and St Andrew's church on Rodney Street. In the foreground is part of the small central gardens which are also owned by the university.

Cleveland Square is named in honour of a former mayor of the city, John Cleveland and is just off Paradise Street close to its junction with Park Lane. Close to the Custom House, docks and city centre this area was badly damaged during the war as can be seen here. In the part of the square on the left would have stood a Chinese Masonic Lodge, the Malakoff Vaults public house and a newsagents. The road that can just be seen on the right was Pitt Street and on the near side of this would have stood a shipping butchers. A shelter that once stood in the centre of the square (bottom) received a direct hit on the night of 31st August/ 1st September 1940 but despite several injuries no-one was killed. The tall warehouse building and those next to it in the background all front onto Argyle street. Between the square and Paradise Street was also an electricity generating station.

Although the square still retains its cobbled surface almost everything else has changed in some way. Modern houses were recently built on the right, cutting off the connection to Pitt Street. On the left a building containing both offices and apartments has been built. The tall warehouse on Argyle Street was retained after the war but has been converted into luxury flats.

St Michael's church was an elegant building which was completed in 1826 and stood in Upper Pitt Street, close to the city's Chinese community and the docks immediately south of the Pierhead. On the night of the 2nd/3rd May 1941 a parachute mine landed in nearby Cornwallis Road which caused serious damage to the surrounding streets and the extensive damage that can be seen here. Four men were awarded the George Medal for their bravery in rescuing a firewatcher from a nearby workshop. They worked for more than an hour to free him despite the fact that the building he was in was in clear danger of collapse.

Due to the extensive damage the church was demolished in 1946. A new church, the rear of which appears in the current photo was built on the site in 1960 along with a small community centre. Much of the old surrounding churchyard was cleared and grassed over.

Taken in the shadow of the Anglican Cathedral this photograph shows the corner of Hardy Street and Grenville Street South. At this point in time the cathedral was still under construction as not even the tower was entirely finished by the time war broke out. Fortunately the cathedral only suffered minor damage, once when a bomb penetrated the roof but deflected out of the building to damage some external stonework, and another time when many of the many of the stained glass windows were broken beyond repair and the founders' plot damaged. The houses in the foreground have suffered from both blast and fire damage. A short distance away is Great George Square where a number of houses were destroyed on the 5th May 1941. Many of the victims in those houses were Merchant Sailors, principally from Belgium, a country which had been occupied by the Nazis. The graves of three of those killed that night can be seen in Anfield Cemetery close to the mass grave site that can be seen on page 151. They are easily identified because each has a Belgian lion at the top.

None of the houses in the foreground are still standing today, allowing us a clear view of the now finished cathedral. The area in front of the cathedral once contained many Georgian properties but these were gradually cleared during the 1960s and 1970s. Modern flats and apartments have since replaced them, but to date nothing has been done with the land in the foreground other than to convert it into grass and erect a small barrier, presumably to prevent it being used as a car park.

The Anglican Cathedral suffered numerous near misses during the war and these often fell in the area off St James Road, causing the kind of damage that can be seen here above. In November 1940 King George VI and Queen Elizabeth toured the city. They observed damage to the cathedral from near the central building in the upper photograph which stood on the corner of St James Road and Washington

Street. They would have had a clear view of the damage to the stained glass windows and the founders' plot. During the visit the King tried to raise morale by giving encouragement and challenging the people of the city to "Keep going, whatever you do, even if you can only go on in a small way".

Since the war most of St James Road has been turned into a car park and the roads off it to the left replaced with modern housing.

Grayson Rollo was one of many ship repair firms with premises close to the docks. These particular premises stood in Bridgewater Street, just a short distance from Wapping Dock. The building was hit by both high explosive and incendiary bombs on the night of 2nd/3rd May 1941. Despite the best efforts of the fire-fighters, including bringing water over from Queen's Dock the building was completely burnt out. The company was especially unfortunate, as their Sandhills premises (below) was hit by 4 high explosive bombs and numerous incendiaries and also badly damaged.

As has been seen the dock road area of the city has seen great changes since the war, making locating comparisons difficult. Only by comparing the building numbers of existing premises on Bridgewater Street was it possible to be certain what side Grayson Rollo's premises once stood on. As can be seen from this photo above the land is now empty and overgrown.

Fisher Street is a small street running off Grafton Street in Toxteth, just opposite the Cains Brewery. On the night of 1st/2nd May 1941 bombs fell on the street and although the shelter in the centre seems to have survived the impact intact there were still some fatalities amongst a group of firewatchers. The edges of shelters built in the centre of a road were frequently painted white to aid drivers during the blackout.

After the war all except one of the houses on Fisher Street were demolished and commercial premises were built here. The street retains its distinctive cobbled surface but it is now closed off by a metal gate making it in effect an alley. The surviving house is at the end of the alley on the right.

This photo shows a badly damaged shelter which stood on the corner of Park Street and Grafton Street in Toxteth. Located close to both Toxteth and Brunswick Docks and the Brunswick Goods Station this area would have suffered greatly from enemy action. This part of Toxteth contained a great many pubs, two of which are shown here. On the left stood the Channel Fleet whose upper windows show a use of crossed tape, an attempt to protect against the glass shattering from bomb impacts. The building on the extreme right was the Mersey View public house which stood across Grafton Street from the Channel Fleet.

The modern view provides us with a stark contrast, with neither public house, nor the surrounding housing having survived. Even Grafton Street is cut short at this point with only a pedestrian path for a short way before continuing on again in the distance. The Mersey View survived until at least the late 1990s but most of the remainder of the area was cleared by then to make way for new housing which can be

seen in the distance and on the right. This clearance now allows us to see all the way to the Anglican Cathedral, whose tower can be seen in the background on the right, dominating the skyline as it does from many places in the city. Where the shelter once stood is now an area of wasteland.

On the night of 17th/18th August 1940 twelve high explosive bombs landed in the vicinity of Brunswick, North Coburg and South Queens Docks. Although they were not the first bombs to fall on Merseyside it was the first raid in which any significant damage was done to a built up area of the city. This view shows the Brunswick Goods Station on the left and on the other side of Caryl Street stands Brunswick Gardens, a five storey tenement block built in 1938. Along with neighbouring Warwick and Caryl Gardens its flats were home to many residents who were lucky to avoid damage from these bombs.

After the war both the Goods Station and Brunswick Gardens were demolished, the former to be replaced by business premises and the latter by a housing development. Caryl Street itself was pedestrianised in many places.

During the night of 12th/13th March 1941 the city suffered one of its heaviest raids to that date. One of the results of that raid can be seen here, where a school once stood. Located on Chatham Place in the Edge Hill district of the city it was a "Special School for Crippled and Mentally Defective Children". The photograph did not appear in the press until more than six months after the raid and details have proved difficult to trace. It is known however that one man named Charles Gwilliams was killed in Chatham Place that night, no doubt whilst carrying his duties as an Air Raid Warden. Nearby at St Anne's School another six men were killed, two of them firewatchers, one an Air Raid Warden and another from the City Police. The number of wardens and watchers who fell in the city during the war belies the popular image such as the interfering cowardly Hodges from *Dad's Army*.

Although Chatham Place still exists the school has now gone. It would have stood behind the railings on the left. It's worth noting that railings were an increasingly rare sight in wartime Britain as they were frequently removed for scrap metal to help in the war effort. Amongst other items recycled were many nineteenth century cannons, themselves a relic of conflicts like the Crimean War. Two of these once stood at the Wavertree Road entrance to the nearby Botanic Gardens. St Anne's church is still standing behind where this photograph was taken.

This photograph shows Stevenson Street which is just off Picton Road in Wavertree. The rubble and bricks in the foreground represent the remains of one of the street shelters, utterly destroyed by a direct hit from a high explosive bomb on the night of the 17th September 1940. In all 8 people were killed on the street that night. Two died in their houses, Maria Burdett at number 87 and Emily Cassidy at number 43. In the shelter in the foreground Charles Eggs, Harry Erdman, Veronica Thomas, Anne Turner, Anthony Turner and Charles Turner were killed. Harry Erdman was just 20 months old and Charles Turner just two years old.

Stevenson Street still retains most of its Victorian houses but here and there are exceptions such as the two seen here on the left. Many years after the war the *Liverpool Echo* asked for people's memories of the war. One reader wrote in to say that they had been a small child playing in Stevenson Street with Harry Erdman just before the raid but when the sirens went sought shelter. The reader went inside their house and survived; Harry went into the shelter and unfortunately did not. At times survival must have seemed a matter of fate or blind luck and this lead many people to shun the shelters, preferring to take their chances in their own home. Most people who lived through the war had a similar tale of fortune to tell.

Many houses suffered lucky near misses such as this one at 21 Green Lane North, Wavertree. Although the bomb cratered the road and shattered the windows no serious damage was done to the building. The gentleman in the crater certainly had a lot of work to do though!

As can be seen from the modern photograph nothing about the property or the quiet suburban road it is located on would ever indicate that it was once the scene of a very narrow escape.

Four people were killed in this area when a high explosive bomb exploded here in the early hours of the 4th May 1941. The bank in the centre of the picture was a branch of the now defunct Martins Bank and stands at the corner of Langdale Road and Smithdown Road. At number 2 Langdale Road Ernest Murphy (aged 49) was killed instantly and although his two sons Dennis (16) and Kevin (14) were rescued from the remains of their house they died later the same day at the David Lewis Northern Hospital. Both Dennis and Ernest were members of the Home Guard. A fourth fatality was William Boardman (29) who lived at 439 Smithdown Road and was also a Home Guard member.

Although the branch of Martins Bank was rebuilt after the war it is no longer a bank. Given the extent of the damage it will come as no surprise to find that the two houses to the left of the bank were replaced with modern housing after the war.

This tangled mess are the remains of Pollard's Garage which was on Ullet Road, opposite Linnet Lane. Taken together with the photograph right it is difficult to believe that the owners could have salvaged much, but the *Daily Mail* caption which accompanied the photograph above assured readers that all the cars were subsequently recovered intact. Presumably there was some delay whilst salvage workers removed the rubble!

After the war the garage operated under the name of Cubbin and North for some time. After this closed the buildings were demolished and the land was turned into a playground for Bellerive School. The buildings in the background of the modern photograph belong to the school.

The church of St
Matthew and St James
stands on a prominent
site off Rose Lane in
Mossley Hill. It was
built between 1870 and
1875. During the night
of 28th/29th August
1940 in one of the
earliest raids on the
city, the church was
badly damaged. This
photograph appeared
in a January *Daily Post*
and shows snow that
has fallen through the
damaged roof.

After the war the
church was rebuilt
between 1950 and 1952
enabling it to remain
in use to this day. Some
of the pillars on the
left still show signs of
damage caused that
night. This view is
towards the church's
altar.

The exterior of St Matthew and St James' church also suffered damage. This photograph was taken some time after the raid and shows repairs under way to the roof. In the foreground are a number of gravestones that make up the garden of rest. They were moved to this position after the raids due to a second bomb having fallen in the grounds creating a 10ft wide crater! On the right is the tower con-taining a clock which stopped at the time of the raid.

The exterior of the church has been repaired making it difficult to imagine that the building was so badly damaged. To the right of where this photograph was taken are a number of interesting graves including one to Pilot Officer Henry Leech. He was sadly killed in a flying accident on the 2nd September 1939.

Local Women at War

THE ROLES of women in wartime Britain were varied and essential to the war effort. The war had meant that many men were away from home on military service, leaving many traditionally male dominated positions in society empty. Women also filled various non-combatant roles within the military. Women did not merely help the war effort though, they had to deal with the consequences of the bombing raids, rationing and regulations that came with home life.

Even before war began the government organised a number of female military organisations to assist the armed forces. Each branch of the armed forces had their own attached organisation, for the Army it was the Auxillary Territorial Services (ATS), for the RAF it was the Women's Auxillary Air Force (WAAFs) and for the Royal Navy it was the Women's Royal Naval Services (WRENS). These organisations would undertake non-combatant roles such as admini-stration, cooking, transport, repair and maintenance of equipment and operation of specialist equipment such as barrage balloons or search lights. The Wrens were especially prominent in the local area due to their work at Western Approaches.

A group of civil defence workers can be seen below near Holy Corner in city centre meeting with the Chief Constable and military commanders. Work did not just have to be through military organisations however, many women moved into jobs in factories and on the land. The Women's Land Army organised people to go to the country to work in the fields planting and gathering crops, or working with animals. For some women this was their first experience of the countryside but most took to it very well. Many travelled as far afield such as Cornwall or Devon, much further than their holidays during the depression years of the 1930s.

The factories also employed women in huge numbers, usually overseen by male foremen and managers. Although this was very dangerous work people were inspired by the knowledge that the faster they turned out weapons or ammunition the better equipped their loved ones on active service would be.

The government would also organise morale boosting exercises such as visits from VIPs or talks from some of the soldiers who used the equipment. One such visit can be seen in the photograph above as the workers greet a returning tank crew.

One other prominent workplace for women was in the hospitals where many were employed as nurses. When war broke out there was a hectic period for them when patients were discharged from the main hospitals in an attempt to free up beds for the expected heavy casualties that fortunately did not occur at that time. With so many hospitals damaged during the war the toll on staff was heavy, and much reliance was placed on volunteers from organisations such as the Red Cross and St John's Ambulance.

The stresses of war had a significant impact on family life, with the men of the household usually away from home, although in ports such as Liverpool many men remained in the city working on the dock system. For most families though the women managed the household, trying to provide for the family whilst coping with the rationing system. Many learnt to improvise in providing unusual food for the family such as rabbit. Others put their skills with needle and thread to good use, for example mending existing clothing to cope.

Through it all the resilience of local women was amazing, with many preferring to concentrate on what they had left rather than what they had lost. Many homeless families soldiered on through the loss of their belongings and house, content that their loved ones were unharmed. Their courage and endurance helped the city survive this dire hour.

Bombed Out!

THE BLITZ on Merseyside did not just wound or kill, it would also damage or destroy properties, making people homeless for long periods whilst alternative housing could be sought. Many people moved in with friends or relatives but others did not have that luxury and were left with no shelter. With these in mind the city set up a network of 70 rest centres throughout the city before the bombing even began. Anyone made homeless was to be directed to these by the local Air Raid Wardens, in some cases transport being provided when an area was particularly badly hit.

Some of these rest centres were fairly basic with little more than camp beds, basic heating and a water supply, others such as the one seen below were reasonably comfortable. When the bombing began in earnest it was soon found that these were inadequate for the sheer number of people whose house had been damaged in the raids. Public buildings such as church halls were taken over and hastily converted to provide similar levels of basic shelter.

These were but temporary solutions to the problems posed by large numbers of homeless families, so other solutions were sought. Newly built council properties were often used and local government also requisitioned unoccupied private property, no doubt to the considerable annoyance of the owners when they returned! Perhaps the most important aspect though was to repair the damaged buildings so that they could be made habitable again.

This work was carried out by the local authority, with an initial investigation carried out as soon as possible after the raid to determine the extent of the damage, followed by immediate "first aid" repairs to prevent the damage from getting worse. This would allow the authorities to save a considerable number of buildings that would otherwise have been demolished or fallen down.

The authorities also helped families by attempting to rescue any furniture found on the site and ensuring that it was moved to the family's new accommodation or placed in storage until it could be used.

Evacuations and Shrapnel – Children at War

FOR THE city's children the war began on the 1st September 1939, even before it was declared. The government, fearing the effects of the enemy bombing of cities had put in place a comprehensive evacuation scheme to move children from the major urban areas to the countryside which began on that day. Children were taken by rail to a central point, often a town or church hall. The photograph below shows children inspecting information about the evacuation. The one on the right shows a group of children on their way to Edge Hill Station.

Local families at the destination would come and choose children that they would take in. Any family that did so received a regular allowance and of course additional rations to feed the extra mouths. Although siblings were kept together where possible this did not always happen and many children got homesick fairly quickly. Although a great many children, disabled people and pregnant women had been evacuated many began to return home. They felt that the lack of enemy air raids was a sign that evacuation had been an unnecessary inconvenience. Shortly after this however the Blitz began and many people found themselves homeless.

Monday morning.....
Please be sure to send your child with a packed bag and the GAS MASK (in box) at 9 o'clock.

Children must come to school this morning and this afternoon as usual.

Scholars will not be taken to the station today. Put what you can in the bags and don't worry.

The raids brought on a second smaller and less formal period of evacuations. Although there were still some government efforts there was also financial support for families who had relations in the countryside to travel there and stay for the duration. Liverpool people were luckier than most in this respect as many had relations in North Wales or rural Lancashire and Cheshire. Evacuation was also promoted through the use of posters with an ARP warden telling a young boy to "leave Hitler to me Sonny".

As the war went on and the raids diminished these too would return home, although for some this meant waiting until they could be re-housed. Experiences of evacuation varied but for many children, brought up in a urban environment this was their first experience of the countryside and they often enjoyed their time such as the children in the photo above, with some not returning to Liverpool until 1944.

For the children that remained behind the city was at times exciting and at others frightening. The heavy raids seemed at times to be a magnet for them, the bombsites providing opportunities to collect pieces of shrapnel as souvenirs or just simply a new place to play, oblivious to the danger many of them must have presented.

Many schools were demolished during the raids giving the pupils an impromptu holiday until alternative arrangements could be found. It remains a sad fact however that despite the attempts at evacuation a large number of children died during the air raids, some of them not even a week old.

The end of the air raids brought a much happier time for the city's children. The entry of America into the war saw a large number of "Yanks" passing through or stationed near the city. They soon became very popular with the local children as they often had chewing gum or chocolate, almost unheard of luxuries in a country still enduring rationing. For the city's children the end of the war and the return to their family slowly brought back normality, although they could be found playing on bombsites for many years to come!

North of the City Centre

THIS SECTION will deal with the area that includes the outskirts of the city centre such as Scotland and Vauxhall Roads and the outlying suburbs such as Dovecot and West Derby. Also included in this section are areas that lie on the border between North and South such as Edge Hill and Old Swan. This area also contained variety, from cramped and unsanitary slums and courts to new housing estates in places like Dovecot. Although sometimes considered less fashionable than the southern half of the city North Liverpool still contains large parks such as Newsham and Stanley and major estates such as Croxteth. The density of population in many areas however made it vulnerable to high casualties when raids began in

Above: Damaged houses on the Dovecot Estate. Below: An example of court dwellings near Burlington Street.

earnest, and many of the biggest incidents of the war occurred in this area.

Close to the junction of Kensington and Low Hill is Holborn Street which mostly comprised narrow three-storeyed Victorian houses. The nearest premises on the left were part of St Jude's School and the first building on the right was part of a chair frame manufacturer's premises. The shelter in the centre of the street was a common sight throughout the city and provided basic protection for those unable to reach a large public shelter or unable to build their own due to a lack of garden.

Holborn Street has been cut short by a modern housing development, so the comparison was taken from further back at the junction with Low Hill in order to give the reader a better point of reference. The building on the right is the former Coach and Horses public house. Built on the site of a much older inn it is now the premises of a radio communication firm. Although

difficult to believe today, Low Hill once represented the boundary of the city of Liverpool, and once a year the mayor and his council would stop at the inn for refreshments during a ride on horseback around the boundary. The building is a rare survivor since the Victorian houses, cobbled street surface, school and business have all long since gone.

Sometimes the caption on a photograph isn't precise enough to know in advance where to take a photograph. In this case someone had written "Leopold Road" next to this photograph in the press cutting from the *Liverpool Echo* dated 5th September 1940. The report stated that "several people received fatal injuries" but the headline preferred to concentrate on the fact that two people in the damaged house on the far left survived and were rescued from their bed. A study of the Commonwealth War Graves Commission records shows that 5 people died in the attack, all from the Birch family. The father Charles would somehow have to pick up the pieces of his shattered life after his wife Margaret (aged 50) and daughters Elsie (20), Christina (17), Winifred (13) and Irene (12) were killed on the night of the 4th September.

Armed with the road name and the knowledge that the photograph showed four houses hit during this particular raid it proved easy to locate the correct part of the road, which is in the Kensington area of the city. The numbers on this side of the road run 75...77...79...85...87, with 77 and 79 being the newer buildings. This shows that 81 and 83 were never rebuilt, the new houses instead being given the luxury of wider frontages and a garage each! The Birch family lived at number 81. Given the angle the original image was clearly taken from the upper floor of one of the buildings on the far side of the road, but this comparison was taken from street level.

of those present losing their lives and many others were seriously injured.

This image shows the desperate rescue attempts that took place over the following days. Although the incident appeared in the local press under the headline "scene of destruction" two days later, the location and scale of the casualties were not mentioned at the time. Even the Prime Minister Winston Churchill commented on the event calling it as "the worst single incident of the war".

After the war a secondary school was built on the site but this closed in the 1980s, the building later reverting to being a college. This building, which stood on the corner of Clint Road and Durning Road

The worst single incident of the whole Blitz in Liverpool occurred on the night of 29th November 1940 when a parachute mine landed on part of the Edge Hill Training College in Durning Road. Part of the building collapsed into the basement shelter below where around 300 people were sheltering. Some of these had only recently arrived in the shelter from trams that had stopped nearby. Boiling water from a damaged heating system and gas from burst mains nearby combined to result in 166

survived until relatively recently when it was demolished and replaced with the housing that can be seen here.

A short distance to the right of where this photograph was taken stands the former Durning Road Fire Station. The engine which fell afoul of a crater in Roe Street came from here. In the background on the left is the tower of Christ Church with St Cyprian's church which was consecrated in July 1881.

place of entertainment in a North West Town after the Nazi night raids". The building featured was the Palace Ice Rink which was on Prescot Road in Fairfield, close to the junction with Beech Street. The exact date that the raid occurred on is not recorded but the police reports do speak of houses being demolished in the Kensington district during the night of 3rd/4th September making this the most likely night.

Its neighbour, the Casino Cinema avoided any serious damage.

The modern comparison shows the junction of Prescot Road (left) and Beech Street (right). The Casino would have been directly behind the hoardings at the corner of the two, the Palace to the left of the Casino. The Palace was later known as the Silver Blades and during the 1970s one of the DJs there was Rory Storm. In the early 1960s his band Rory Storm and the Hurricanes included a pre-Beatles Ringo Starr on drums. After numerous changes of ownership the rink closed for good in 1986 and was demolished in 1990 leaving Merseyside sadly without a rink.

This image appeared in the *Liverpool Post* on the 7th September 1940 captioned "The damaged roof of a

This photograph shows the St George pub on Green Lane in Old Swan. This was the second pub of this name on the site and was popular with American troops stationed in the area as they used it to court local women. According to the newspaper cutting two people died here. No date was given for the photograph but the Green Lane area was badly hit during September 1940. On the night of the 4th/5th a police report noted that the nearby Lister Drive Power Station seemed to be an enemy target. Although no damage was inflicted on the power station the report noted that some was inflicted on the surrounding properties.

Later on the 17th September 8 Auxiliary firemen were killed in the Emergency Fire Station on Green Lane. The power station was a big building with four large chimney stacks making it an obvious target. During one of the attacks on the power station a near miss hit a nearby stack of coal sending large chunks of the rationed fuel raining down on the local area. It will come as no surprise to find that not much of that coal was ever recovered! Green Lane also contained a Corporation Water Works making it an important area for maintaining basic amenities to the rest of the city.

The new St George pub was built on the same site in 1957. The new building was set back from the road slightly to allow for the addition of a car park.

Located just off Green Lane in Tuebrook, Brainerd Street was typical of many of the streets in this part of the city. This view looks away from Green Lane towards Newsham Park where the tower of the former Seaman's Orphanage can be seen in the distance. On the left hand side of the street were three shelters that were constructed between January and March 1940. This type was a public rather than private shelter, designed with rows of benches, electric lights and both male and female lavatories! They were a far cry from the brick-built street corporation shelters like the one below, left. This one was in Radcliffe Street in Everton and is seen during a visit by the Lord Mayor, Alderman Sir Sydney Jones and Alderman Shennan. Although this type looks basic in reality both types on this page were effective at saving lives since they would withstand most things short of a direct hit.

The wasteland on the left hand side of Brainerd Street was built on after the war, being replaced by a care home and flats. This makes direct comparison impossible. The former Seaman's Orphanage still stands in the distance.

This photograph was printed in the *Liverpool Post* for August 31st 1940 and talks of a "new hotel in the suburbs of a North Western town". This vague reference to the target town was part of a government plan to avoid giving intelligence to the enemy about the accuracy of their raids. Although the government had originally stated that large cities such as Liverpool and London would be exempted from the plan

newspapers generally didn't refer to Liverpool or Merseyside by name until late September. Even after this date smaller local areas such as Birkenhead or Bootle were often only referred to as "Merseyside" rather than being specific. Both the local and national press would eventually give the city the coverage it was due but for many the plan backfired. It had a negative effect on civilian morale since locals felt that their bravery and fortitude was being ignored in favour of cities such as London. Despite this change of reporting the myth of a "North Western town" stuck, not helped by the fact that the bombing of the city did not feature once in the wartime newsreels, unlike Manchester, Coventry or London.

The "hotel" was the Jolly Miller pub which stands on the corner of Queen's Drive and Mill lane on the outskirts of West Derby. Only a small corner of the building was damaged by the bombing raid and strangely none of the windows were shattered by the explosion. The corner was rebuilt shortly after the war, allowing the building to retain a similar exterior appearance despite the passage of more than 70 years.

Even Liverpool's outlying suburbs were not immune to damage from the occasional raid as this photograph of a house in Dovecot shows. The building, which stands on the corner of Swanside Road and Pilch Lane, is typical of the type of housing which was built throughout the Dovecot Estate in the early 1930s. Prior to this it was a quiet rural area with the occasional estate or mansion. The raid which wrecked the house so badly took place on 30th August 1940. Despite the extensive damage to the front of the building no-one was injured either there or in the house on the left where the windows have been shattered. Houses with gardens such as this one would often build Anderson shelters in them. As the photograph bottom shows they were very

sturdy, some even surviving a house collapsing on them!

Such shelters were quick and easy to build by the owners with materials such as the corrugated metal provided for them by the authorities. Households without a garden or cellar could either go to communal shelters or construct a Morrison shelter, a steel topped design resembling a table.

Since the war the house on the right has been rebuilt in a similar style. The people living here now probably have no idea that the previous owners had such a near miss!

This wartime photograph above shows Scotland Place on the left and Richmond Row on the right. Although taken in January 1944 the bomb damage has not been repaired. The building on the far left was the old Morning Star public house. A former tenant of the pub called Patrick Byrne renovated the building and it became a very popular place making him enough money to purchase several properties in the region. He was often involved in assisting the poor of the area and especially local dock workers. Sadly the man known as "Dandy Pat" died aged just 45 in 1890. A drinking fountain was erected in his memory and can just be seen on the left opposite the pub.

The Morning Star was the last surviving pub (of three) on Scotland Place but was eventually demolished in the early 1960s. The whole area was soon irrevocably altered by the building of the Wallasey Tunnel. Richmond Row no longer connects to this area which is now part of Byrom Street and as the road layout makes a direct comparison impossible, the photograph (right) shows

the general area. The buildings on the right are part of the University of Liverpool. The Patrick Byrne statue remained in place until the 1970s when it was moved to Pownall Square (by the site of St Mary's church on page 50). After being vandalised in the 1980s its whereabouts were unknown until a committee managed to locate the plinth in a yard owned by the council. This was later restored and relocated to St Anthony's church on Scotland Road.

This photograph shows the stretch of Scotland Road between Mile End and Hornby Street. Although it appears at first glance to show a cratered street surface in the foreground in reality buildings once stood there in a triangular patch of land between Scotland Road and Cazneau Street. This area once contained a public library and a drapery firm. The photo was probably taken shortly after the raid which caused the damage since only a temporary barrier of rope strung between posts has been erected and men are still hard at work clearing up the mess. The buildings in the background have all suffered blast damage from the raid.

As has already been mentioned the Scotland Road area is hardly recognisable since the construction of the Kingsway Tunnel in the 1970s and an exit road for this is on the left. A road on the left retains the name of Mile End but Hornby Street has been replaced by the much shorter Raymond Place which is on the right. The shops that appear in the wartime photograph have been demolished and replaced by the modern housing that can be seen in the background. The buildings that once stood in the foreground were never rebuilt, and Cazneau Street is now only a short minor road, cut off from Scotland Road by another tunnel approach road. Virgil Street (see page 147) would once have ran out into Scotland Road just to the left of here.

Located at the junction of Scotland Road and Stanley Road the Rotunda Theatre was a famous landmark in this part of the city. In addition to the theatre the building also contained a public house, the Rotunda Vaults which the actors usually frequented. The building was badly damaged by fire during the night of 4th/5th May 1941 and around 2am a large part of the building collapsed. Although it appeared in print in 1942 this photograph was presumably taken shortly after the collapse.

After the war the area that the Rotunda once occupied was cleared and later converted into a traffic island that some locals still refer to as the Rotunda today.

Virgil Street once ran between Scotland Road and Great Homer Street and consisted almost entirely of residential properties. Near the junction with Scotland Road also stood one of the city's infamous courts, poor quality cramped houses that were sometimes only dignified with a number rather than a name. The court would have been on the left in this photograph. The damage seen here was inflicted on the night of the 9th/10th January 1941.

After the war Virgil Street, like so many others in the area changed so much that it is hardly recognisable today. The slum clearances of the '60s and '70s were followed by the construction of the Wallasey Tunnel in 1971. Approach roads for the tunnel now run on the right, cutting off the route to Scotland Road for vehicles. Like much of the area the residential properties have gone, replaced in this case by builders' merchants, a garage and other commercial premises.

Nothing but memories and photographs remain to indicate that people once lived here, although the cobbled street surface mostly remains. In this photo Scotland Road is behind the camera, Great Homer Street in the distance.

Bidder Street once ran from Islington to Langsdale Street, parallel to Birchfield Street on the next page. The photograph (top) was taken in 1945 when street shelters such as these were totally redundant and would be soon removed.

The presence of landed flats on the left suggests that this photograph was taken from the Islington end of the street.

Although a modern day Bidder Street exists in this area its alignment and location are completely different. It now runs roughly parallel to Islington on the far side of Langsdale Street from the original. This can be seen in the photograph above right. The site of the old Street would have been in the centre of the photograph above left, through the back gardens of these modern houses.

This wartime photograph shows the view along Birchfield Street which runs from Islington to Langsdale Street. It is interesting to note that the street shelter in the centre of the street almost completely blocks passage along the street, an indication perhaps of how comparatively little traffic used this route even before the war. A close study of post-war pictures reveals the building seen on the left to be the "Birchfield" public house which stood on the corner of Islington and Birchfield Street. Ever resourceful, the local children have chalked cricket stumps onto the wall of the shelter. Birchfield Street is named after a series of three houses built there, one of which was once occupied by William Roscoe, a historian, botanist and anti-slavery activist. For a brief period he was also MP for one of the city's two seats and in this role he helped see the passing of a bill for the abolition of the slave trade in 1807. This was a considerable achievement as Liverpool had played a major part in the trade for more than half a century. It is estimated that a total of three million Africans were transported across the Atlantic on Liverpool registered ships.

The area of Islington is yet another part of North Liverpool that has changed so much as to be nearly unrecognisable today. Unlike Bidder Street on the previous page, Birchfield retained its alignment and length but the mix of Victorian terraces and landed flats have been swept away in favour of these modern houses. The pub lasted until the early 1970s when most of that side of Islington was demolished.

Mill Road Infirmary stood just off the junction between Mill Road and Caird Street. Originally built as a workhouse for the sick poor by the West Derby Board of Guardians it was renamed an Infirmary in 1891. From that point up to the war it acted as a general hospital. On the night of 3rd/4th May 1941 a mine exploded between C and E blocks demolishing both. In an emergency operating theatre under one of these a Greek Seaman was already anaesthetised and had his stomach opened as part of the operation which was well underway when the air raid sirens went off. The surgeon elected to continue but the mine caused the roof of the basement to fall in. Rescuers managed to free the staff that had been present but the patient was trapped by a slab of concrete. Eventually he was also freed and he went on to a complete recovery after completing his operation at Walton Hospital. Most of the building was put out of action in this single night and over 80 people were killed, but the prompt reaction of the rescue squads in freeing those trapped and the ambulance service in transferring patients to other hospitals kept this total lower than it might have been.

After the war the hospital was rebuilt and turned into a maternity unit. It remained in use until the early 1990s when the new Liverpool Women's Hospital was built and was demolished shortly after. New housing occupies the site of the hospital but an external wall remains to the rear of the house on the far left of this modern view.

On the 5th December 1940 a mass funeral was held at Anfield Cemetery attended by clergy from the Protestant and Catholic faiths, the Lord Mayor and civic dignitaries. A guard of honour was provided by the police, nurses and every section of the Civil Defence forces. Most of the 504 bodies buried here were unidentified victims. This photograph shows mourners passing the graves, a process that took several hours according to the next day's *Liverpool Post*. In May 1941 a further 1,000 bodies were buried in the cemetery. After the war the city erected a monument to those buried in the mass grave which can be seen left middle. It bears the city's coat of arms and an inscription in memory of those who lost their lives. A short distance away from the mass grave are three graves (bottom) that stand out due to their inscriptions being in a foreign language. These are the final resting places of two seamen and one officer of the Belgian Merchant Navy who were killed on the 5th May 1941.

The top photograph has been labelled as 37/39 Borwen Street, Anfield but no such street exists. There is however a Corwen Road and a visit there confirmed that this was the correct location. As can be seen both buildings were very badly damaged with most of the external walls destroyed and the chimney stack destroyed but the bath and one bed seem to have survived intact. Fortunately no-one seems to have been killed in this raid which occurred sometime in August 1940. At this date casualties were still low although lists of them naturally drew crowds eager for news of friends or relatives in other areas of the city. This can be seen from the photograph below where the progress towards the War Weapons Week target for October 1940 is completely ignored.

Both 37 and 39 Corwen Road seem to have been rebuilt since the war and there is no remaining indication that either suffered such heavy damage.

When this photograph of damaged houses appeared in the press on the 2nd September 1940 it was reported only as being from a raid on a North-Western area in the last two days. Fortunately a note in the record offices identified it as showing Edge Lane opposite the Pexwear factory. According to the Gores Directory for 1938 this factory stood opposite Douro Place and manufactured overalls. Thomas Woosey and Jack Chambers, both Air Raid Wardens along with two civilians, Jack Mooney and Edwin Stephenson were injured in Edge Lane but sadly all died later of their wounds in Broadgreen Hospital. Whilst it cannot be certain where in Edge Lane these injuries took place the extensive damage to these buildings certainly would not rule out this particular area. Edge Lane was also home to the Littlewoods Pools premises which were turned over to the war effort. It became home to MC5, the government's post censorship service which employed around 2,000 staff. Their role was to monitor up to 100,000 items of post a day, keeping a vigilant watch for attempts by enemy agents to communicate with Germany or sympathisers with each other. Littlewoods also turned over their Walton Hall Avenue factory to the production of Wellington Bombers.

Since the war this area of Edge Lane has changed dramatically. The housing has long since been cleared away and replaced by business premises and a retail park. Since there was no exact location for the houses it is difficult to be precise, but this is the area opposite the site of the former Pexwear factory.

Football

SPORT HAS always played a major part in British people's lives and Liverpool's two big clubs are arguably the best followed of them all. Unfortunately for the fans the war severely curtailed football matches almost from the moment it was declared. On the 14th September 1939 the government announced that games would continue but travel restrictions put into place meant that the national league had to be abandoned as no team could travel more than 50 miles. Fortunately for the city the two clubs are just a short distance across Stanley Park from each other.

The government also limited attendances to just 8,000 out of fears that a bombing raid would occur during a game. Whilst this is still a large number of people in one place it was but a fraction of the normal attendance which in the 1930s regularly topped 50,000 for a Merseyside Derby. Although the limit was later raised to 15,000 many people still missed out. Many players were also called up to serve in the military and this reduced the quality of the leagues that did take place. One of these players was Matt Busby who joined Liverpool in 1936 but is now better known for managing Manchester United in the '50s and '60s. He missed several games due to military service.

One fixture that featured regularly was the Merseyside Derby with the two clubs meeting up to seven times a year. As the war went on the limits on attendances were relaxed and had returned to their pre war numbers by the final year of the war. Matches also continued to be played despite bomb damage such as that seen in the photograph below which shows one of the stands at Goodison Park, the home of Everton FC.

During the war Goodison Park was also used by an American Forces baseball league and as a barrage balloon anti-aircraft post. Liverpool FC's home, Anfield on the other hand hosted boxing matches throughout the war, helping to entertain troops and locals alike.

Prisoners Under Attack

FOR THE inmates of Walton Jail it could almost be argued there was no need for air raid shelters. Built in 1855 the building was a prime example of a solid Victorian prison with thick stone walls that would protect those inside from much of the affects of an air raid. Over 600 prisoners were housed in the jail at any one time during the war. Sadly for those people incarcerated within its walls the prison was not immune to the effects of Goering's planes and some did die during the war.

On the night of the 18th September 1940 bombs hit "K" wing, damaging the masonry there and shattering a gas main. The dust from the masonry and gas hampered rescue attempts but some prisoners were dug out of the rubble and recovered from their ordeal.

The prison was next hit on that terrible night of the 3rd May 1941, this time receiving no less than 8 direct hits that killed 22 prisoners. Of these 10 were adults killed in "I" wing and 12 classed as younger prisoners, killed in "D" wing. Two of the number were interned aliens. Other bombs peppered the remaining blocks, including one that landed in the remains of "K" wing doing little damage to what rubble remained. One prisoner thought to have been killed in the bombings was later found to have escaped but was soon recaptured.

The guards and prison personnel acted bravely, tending to the wounded and recovering the dead whilst ensuring that the prison remained largely secure. The damage was too great however and the prison was no longer operable as a secure unit. Prisoners were transferred either to Strangeways in Manchester or Stafford Prison. Many of the prison officers were decorated for their bravery on the two nights.

A strange postscript to the events at the jail occurred in 1952 when prisoners clearing the debris of "I" wing found the remains of a body that had no hands or feet. Whilst the inquest returned a verdict that the body was that of a prisoner killed on the night of the 3rd of May no-one was able to adequately explain why the prison authorities had already accounted for all the prisoners on their roll. Just who the prisoner was therefore remains a mystery.

The End

THE WAR in Europe officially came to an end on the 8th May 1945 with Germany's unconditional surrender. The war against Japan came to an end on the 15th August when Japan surrendered after the dropping of atomic bombs on two of her cities. After nearly six years of titanic struggle the war was finally over, and people were eager to celebrate. People came out onto the streets, crowding the city centre as can be seen on page 77. People also took part in street parties similar to those seen for coronation or jubilee celebrations in more recent times.

Times were still austere though as rationing was still very much a feature of everyday life. For many serving in the military the end of the war did not mean a return home was imminent. Many remained in the forces for a year or more before being "demobbed" and returned to civilian life. Many received some basic training in a trade such as bricklaying and everyone received a new suit. Armed with these Merseyside's men folk returned to civilian life and a city that had been battered whilst they were away but remained unbeaten.

Also passing through the city were a large number of repatriated people returning from prisoner of war camps both in Europe and Asia. Many of these people were in a poor state of health and needed constant medical care so returned home on hospital ships, often liners converted for the purpose such as the neutral Swedish ship *Drottningholm* seen below.

During the war there was a possibility that even hospital ships might have been mistaken for carrying wounded military personnel and attacked. In an attempt to avoid this, ships from neutral nations such as Sweden were often used. On ships like these hundreds of thousands of soldiers and displaced civilians passed through the port on their way to post-war life.

With the return of the repatriated civilians and wounded armed forces personnel Liverpool's war could finally be said to have come to a close. The results however were still very much in evidence across the city. Some bomb sites would remain unoccupied for decades after the war, used as temporary car parks or gardens for office workers. For the lucky few they would only be reminded of what was missing when passing an empty plot of land. For most they could recall only too well relatives or friends who did not live to see the victory that their hard work had helped to achieve. In memory of those people many local communities erected simple memorials such as the one on this page which stands near to the site of where Blackstock Gardens stood.

The city would recover from her terrible ordeal, and still to this day remains part of a major port system through the container dock at Seaforth. It has endured hard times since the war such as the unemployment and riots of the 1980s but has come through it all. In 2008 it was nominated as European Capital of Culture, surprising many outsiders, but those who

visited found a diverse and interesting city that had much more to offer than the Beatles and two famous football clubs. This has only been possible because of the bravery, skill and dedication of the men, women and even children who went through those dark two years from August 1940 onwards. To them we all owe a debt beyond our capacity to ever repay.

Today's Europe is a very different place from that of 1939 with much closer co-operation between countries, especially within the European Union. One aspect of this is that cities and towns are often twinned with another in a different country that it shares common traits or experiences with. In Liverpool's case it has been twinned with Cologne since 1952. Cologne was also badly damaged during the war with over 70% of the city's buildings effectively destroyed and its famous Dom Cathedral badly damaged. Like Liverpool, Cologne also rebuilt itself, rising like a phoenix from the flames. If we are fortunate this willingness to concentrate on what unites rather than divides us will mean that no city ever has to do so again.

Index

Bold page numbers refer to photographs. Italic page numbers indicate maps. Numbers in bold italics indicate both text and photograph on the page. Text in italic denotes ships and works of art. Parenthesis (curved brackets) are used for clarity.